"The go-to book if you want to understand what permissioned blockchains can do for you."

Professor Gur Huberman, Robert G. Kirby Professor of Behavioral Finance, Columbia Business School

"Wow, very well done…powerful and interesting. Trust and transparency is what you get from *[Block]Chain*."

Anouk Brumfield, Global Blockchain Services Leader, IBM

"Makes eminent sense…could not be more timely…with Covid dispersing talent. Will the real Satoshi please stand up!"

Jake Thomas, Williams Brothers Professor of Accounting and Finance, School of Management, Yale University

"Elizebeth brilliantly outlines how blockchain-based solutions will allow for trusted, validated access to information around skills, experience, as well as projects and job opportunities, controlled and distributed by the individual—engendering trust and accelerating the kind of collaboration which will help individuals and organizations transform to meet these turbulent times. Elizebeth's book crisply and thoughtfully delineates the roadmap of this critical infrastructure for the transformation of the way we all work."

Mark Arian, CEO of Korn Ferry
Consulting

"Elizebeth Varghese has always been a deep thinker, futurist, and strong consultant. Expertly fusing personal experiences with the potential of blockchain technology, Elizebeth provides a vivid picture and roadmap to transform the complex, confusing, and cumbersome world of managing talent. Fascinating."

Robert Gandossy, PhD, Global
Advisor and Strategist, Thought
Leader, Author, and President of
Gandossy Consulting

"Blockchain is essential in the information age as a digital tool to make knowledge productive. This outstanding book demystifies blockchain, shows its many applications, especially to assure human capital for the future, and will become THE reference guide for its use."

Dave Ulrich, Rensis Likert Professor, Ross School of Business, University of Michigan Partner, The RBL Group

"In her ground-breaking new book, Elizebeth calls on leaders and talent evangelists to usher in a new age of connection and collaboration with blockchain technology. Insightful and easily understood, [Block]Chain Reaction teaches the technical ins and outs of this technology, while showing how it can be used to transform the way we hire, retain, and utilize the talent in our businesses. Emerging at the front of a new frontier in talent management, this book will help you thrive in today's rapidly changing world."

Marshall Goldsmith, New York Times #1 Bestselling Author of *Triggers, Mojo, and What Got You Here Won't Get You There*

"To many people, blockchain might sound like a mystifying and menacing word, signifying the swampy and dangerous virtual swirling waters where nothing is real except the sharks and leeches ready to take your finances on a wild, destructive ride. Not a bit of it! In this wonderfully humane and intelligent book, Elizebeth Varghese lucidly demystifies the blockchain methodology and points the way to safer and more efficient future transacting, eliminating the intermediary leeches and protecting against the phony sharks. In a highly personal and most engaging narrative, this talented scholar shows the transformational potential of blockchain beyond the domain of finance—in learning, recruiting, and areas of decision-making where we want fast and reliable guarantees of fidelity. This terrific book is timely, invigorating, and above all, a cause for optimism."

Nigel Nicholson, Evolutionary Psychologist, Emeritus Professor of Organisational Behaviour at the London Business School, and Author of *The 'I' of Leadership: Strategies for Seeing, Being and Doing*

"This is the intersection between technology, ethics, and talent—the best of science and art.

"Varghese starts to uncover and establish the future of organizational optimization, which has huge implications across all sectors, especially in space security and exploration (which she touches upon).

"Varghese breaks down blockchain for the layperson and explains how this emerging technology presents a unique opportunity for organizations to counter cognitive biases and securely apply the right talent to the right place, structure, and time. She draws upon her own experiences and values to show how blockchain breaks through common barriers to efficiency and access, while presenting a theory of how to keep an organization ahead of the competition with technology-empowered, responsible governance."

Dr. Raj Agrawal, Graduate Professor
and 20-year US Defense Sector
Professional, US Space Force

"Excellent effort and pathbreaking conceptualization of emerging ecosystem and data vulnerability for appreciating blockchain in different managerial verticals that are highly appreciable. The author's insights for synchronization of functional nodes to provide transparency and enhanced security through blockchain conceptual framework will be helpful to all organizational stakeholders. The book will reinforce strategic options and provide trust and reliable data management capability across organizations."

Dr. Abhijit Gangopadhyay, Professor
& Dean of the Aegis School Of
Business, Data Science &
Telecommunication

[BLOCK]CHAIN REACTION

The Future of How We Live and Work

ELIZEBETH VARGHESE

Contents

For
Chinnu and Moni,

you inspire us to stay "Forever Young"[1]

asato mā sadgamaya
tamasomā jyotir gamaya[1]

From ignorance, lead me to truth
From darkness, lead me to light

Introduction

This book has been many years in the writing. The premise for the Universal Talent Exchange grew from a kernel of insight as I observed how opportunities are accessed in the world of work and life. Much like my own journey—it started in India, then continued to find resonance in multiple, unexpected places. Then, melding, remembering, committing—it made its way over the past five years, into articles, podcasts, speeches, presentations and now finally, as this book.

About three years ago, I spoke on the topic of Blockchain in Talent, at a national technology and innovation event. I was allotted a speaking slot that conflicted with a keynote, and at a different building across the green. I was unfazed as I was used to the puzzled looks at this topic.

But, then it started to rain. The feathery San Francisco drizzle colored my walk into a cold, gray misery. I sped up, umbrella-less, worrying what the rain could do to my laptop. Regret at my new footwear grew when squelching water made the shoes pinch.

Now, I remember this so vividly because, when I got there, there was a surprising number in the audience, all who had also braved the insidious rain. My sodden spirits lifted as I looked up into the dim auditorium with stadium seating, rising up from the floor where I stood. I sensed energy. Interest. There were so many questions. Some, from those disenchanted by the unilateral crypto-narrative on the technology. Many, from people curious about *what else* blockchain could do.

Fast forward to today. In some ways, we are still there—looking outward from the bright floor of a darkened theater. But, in some very important ways, we *have* moved forward. And, we stand at the inflection point to trigger much more, significant momentum. To hear more about where we are, and where we are headed, read on.

Your focus may be to wield technology to change business and strategy plot lines. Or your focus may be on blockchain and its implications on the talent ecosystem. You may be a blockchain enthusiast curious about its applications outside the realm of crypto and finance. You may be an expert and commentator on the changing nature of leadership, skills, talent in the global arena. You may be an expert on optimizing HR processes and data. Or you may seek to democratize access to opportunities and tap into universal potential. This book provides a view on how the intentional use of this technology can help us all.

I hope this book inspires entrepreneurs and technology enthusiasts everywhere to learn more about blockchain. And, ultimately, brings together minds everywhere, to trust and work in sync—to uncover all potential by connecting in the Universal Talent Exchange.

Elizabeth Varghese
January 5, 2022
New York, New York

Acknowledgments

I am grateful for the inspiration and encouragement from my husband, Mathew, our girls, Aanika and Lara, my parents, Dr. Chinnamma Varghese and Dr. Varghese Abraham, and my sisters. Special thanks to Anu who helped with the title, design, and spent many hours reviewing and correcting the manuscript. I'm also very grateful to Mummy and Daddy, who have been steadfast in their support over the years.

Thank you to my teachers at the Tata Institute of Social Sciences—especially Dr. Ramesh C. Datta who helped us see the intersectionality of success and access.

Dr. Sudhakar Shinde and Monika Navandar— thank you for the gift of time and for being such inspiring role models.

The stories and incidents in this book are all true, though names have been changed. There are many more unknown and untold stories, and unwritten ones that didn't make it into this book. I acknowledge the journeys and courage in all.

Sincere thanks to Professor Gur Huberman of Columbia Business School for his review and coaching. I also thank Amy Wright and IBM for the support, and acknowledge the IBM blockchain team led by Anouk Brumfield.

Many friends reviewed chapters and gave me input, feedback, and important things to consider. Thank you, Marina, Anjali, Shalini, Archana, TVR, Sagar, Siddharth, Rima, Keerthi, Neelima, Sonia, Anu, and Radhika.

I'm very thankful to my publisher, Kayleigh O'Keefe, and the entire publishing team at Soul Excellence for the impetus and support to finally put this down.

My dawn and weekend writing companion is Chutney Theodore, our intrepid Yorkie. Chutney is a five-pound cheerleader and taskmaster who keeps me company by my desk, wakes up to chase away birds from the window, and protests loudly when I stop writing and leave the room.

This was not a convenient time to write a book. I'm lucky beyond measure to have so many people rooting for me to get this out of the door. I wouldn't have buckled down to write this without my ecosystem of support and friendship across the world.

My friends help me become a better person every day, and you all made this book better as well.

ONE

Our Connected Future

OUR WORLD IS SHRINKING, while the universe of knowledge is expanding.

Think about the changes that have unfolded in the past one hundred years. Even within the past fifty years. Or what we have seen—even just in your and my lifetimes.

In the 1960s, my parents moved to Bombay from their villages in Kerala. They were the first generation to come of age in the newly independent India. Invigorated by self-sovereignty and the victory over centuries of foreign rule, they glittered with hope, with clarity. Moni and Chinnu chose to stay in India and build a new day, wielding science and technology.

Moni, Chinnu, and many other young people looked ahead, left their villages (many still shackled by the stains of colonialism), and swarmed out into the world. They shone with heady confidence to be their own people in their own country, to own their destiny, and to build their own nation.

Raising their family among the teeming millions of Bombay,[1] Moni and Chinnu wrote letters home. Many letters, on light blue "inland" paper, folded over and pasted with curved flaps. Each letter from my "Ammachi" (grandmother) traveled from an island on the Meenachil river in Kerala,[2] where Moni grew up. The beautiful Meenachil, which snakes along the coast, is a treacherous neighbor. She floods her banks every year, giving but also taking back—lives, land, dreams—each time. There was only one way across. Everything —people, clothes, livestock, (except my grandfather's Ford Model-T, which had to be parked on the mainland)—went over with the *valla-karan* (boatman) who used a long bamboo pole to push the boat across the water. If the *vallam* (boat) stayed seamless, and the *valla-karan* sober, everything went over as planned.

The letters traveled across the water and then went by train up the Konkan coast. They usually took a week, much longer in the monsoons, to get to Bombay. The letters and replies often overlapped and didn't always arrive in sequence. Questions asked in one letter were sometimes preempted by another or remained unanswered. As the summer months approached, this exchange of letters would intensify in dizzying preparation for the long journey back home.

Finally, with the dates locked down, tickets booked and confirmed, the annual pilgrimage to Kerala would begin. Moni and Chinnu, with their squabbling brood, needed three days and two nights to go home. They traveled on the Jayanti Janata (literally "Victorious People") train, which ambled through five states in the dusty, parched, Indian summer.

The datasets were not standardized, the exchange protocols were inconsistent, the networks and power supply were unreliable, the technology was rudimentary, but the human spirit fueled everything. It fueled the explosion of reach, the urge for access, the push to achieve.

Means of transportation, conducting business, and sharing information have changed how we live and work. We are no longer confined to a small circle, our own neighborhoods, and villages, for our jobs or our personal networks. Thanks to air travel, cars, and developed transportation systems and infrastructure, we can go as far as we want with relative speed. And this extent of our reach continues to grow. As you recall what you hear about commercial space exploration these days, consider our slow but inevitable migration to extra-planetary life and work (more to come on this).

We can certainly go much farther, much faster than before. And yet, we don't have to go far at all to live easier, potentially better lives. We don't have to go any farther than our computer, or even the phone in our pocket, to do business or socialize with someone across the globe. Connection and opportunity are as close as our fingertips. And connectivity not just with who we interact with but to a universe full of possibility.

So how do we navigate this brave new world? How do we engender trust, functional trust that helps us live and work?

Our barrier to operating seamlessly lies in how we trust each other as we share and exchange information about our lives, our credentials, our contributions. And as we work together across geographical boundaries, the next revolution is in trusting each other in our connectivity.

And trust is then the biggest need and enabler to work together across the world.

Now, even as you read this, three rapidly evolving developments grow in influence. Fueled and driven by technology, they snowball and entangle as they unfold. They will change how we live, work. And trust.

First, the rise of *quantum computing* with its impact on data processing and encryption.[3] Second, the speed of *space exploration* with its implications on industry, geopolitics, security and, very remote work.[4] Third, the origami horizons of the *Metaverse*.[5] More on all these in Chapter 4.

Each of these developments accelerates and alters our ability to connect. All magnify the need for real trust.

Not since Nikolai Tesla toyed with the idea of a "world wireless system" (eventually becoming what we know as the internet[6]), in the early 1900s, has any technology held as much potential to transform the way we connect and trust each other. Like the internet, though, not everyone immediately saw the value or the vision. It was an unknown, untapped arena at first. Now it's ubiquitous. Blockchain, I believe, will follow a similar trajectory. My hope in inviting you into this conversation is to demystify this next step in our human connection.

We need to disrupt aspiration, access, and opportunity. The need for this spans far more than our work lives, but we can start there because it's ripe for disruption and it's familiar. It's critical to solve so that we can unleash the potential of all people —no matter where they live.

Like my parents in the 1960s (and perhaps yours), the opportunity to shift, grow upwards, and outwards remains limited, even today. I see it even on the island of Manhattan where we are raising our family. The barriers to cross onto the island remain. The hurdles to transcend neighborhoods, into safer ones with better schools, remain. And for every great success story of transcendence, there are many lost ones. For every Shawn Carter, Jennifer Lopez, and Alex Rodriguez, there are many more who fall into the chasm of Rikers Island. Even today, access to connection and opportunity remain selective, tenuous, and subject to vagaries.

We've all experienced the process of trying to capture an entire career, accomplishments, and educational background onto a resume or CV. Most of us have experienced the challenges of reaching out for opportunities. Many of us may have struggled to find the right job that matches our skills and aspirations.

And too many have stayed unemployed after being impacted by a layoff or a downturn—highly skilled and motivated, but unemployed.

Those of us who hold managerial or executive roles understand the importance of bringing the right people onto the team. We know the frustrations and challenges of recruiting and retaining talent in an increasingly dynamic business climate. We know how difficult it is to find the right person with the right skills and to help them grow and develop.

Additionally, with the continuous business disruption we see these days, the skills required to pivot with strategy are constantly changing. Organizations increasingly recognize that you can't let go of employees and rehire each time for new skills. Instead, you have to reskill, upskill, and tap into the ecosystem of talent that is available on-demand. It's no longer about hiring and developing people; it's about tapping into the entire talent ecosystem, inside and outside the organization.

These talent ecosystems are the perfect arena for a blockchain enablement. They involve high levels of human interaction, record-keeping, and often manual sifting—and that's in addition to cumbersome and time-consuming verification processes. Imagine a technology that does all the streamlining and verification for you, in a trustworthy, secure manner. This will allow focus on matching the exact right candidates for each job and identifying people who've demonstrated that they have the new and emerging sets of skills needed. Imagine a process that could take the heavy lifting out of maintaining, overseeing, and paying contingent workers so you could save money, avoid disputes and reconciliations, and shift your valuable resources elsewhere. Imagine being able to tap into a far broader field of talent and living up to your goals of a more equitable hiring process. Imagine finding the best person—no matter where they sit—in terms of geography, levels of privilege, or access.

You don't have to imagine. All of these possibilities already exist; they just need to be refined and widely embraced. We are in the early stages of a revolutionary change in how we interact, how we control our digital identities and destinies, and how we exchange goods and services—a function that has been part of our society since the dawn of human civilization. This is a new beginning.

Talent and Human Potential: The Engine for Progress

Talent and people are being watched more closely than they ever have been before. In addition to an increased focus on intentional inclusion and diversity in hiring and promotions, generational shifts push more employees to switch jobs more often. The old paradigm where workers would put in forty years in exchange for steady pay and pension is gone. Employees want to be compensated fairly, but they also want flexibility, purpose, and challenges. They want environments that are forward-thinking and offer opportunity. Many are shifting to gig work so they can take the reins of their career and their talent wherever they wish, whenever they want. The core challenge to talent managers is still to find the right fit. It's also challenging to hold on to those right-fit employees and be able to move swiftly when an employee is promoted, makes a lateral move, or wants to switch to the next job at a different company. The global talent exchange, which we'll discuss, brings a wealth of candidates, but the sheer amount of information is a complex puzzle for even the best trained artificial intelligence (AI). And, if not well constructed, AI can come with built-in bias.

The evolving demands of employees and potential employees, the staggeringly speedy changes in the marketplace and skills gaps that come with them, and the massive data overload all combine to exacerbate the difficulties of finding, verifying, and hiring the right candidates. That's where blockchain comes in with answers and cost savings. Recent studies[7] predict that blockchain will reduce back-office costs by at least 20 percent, perhaps up to 30 percent.[8] With talent acquisition costs running around $4,500 per hire and over 100 million people employed, hiring is now a $730+ billion industry. If you do the math to calculate a 25 percent savings on those numbers, we're looking at industry-wide returns of over $200 billion in cost savings. According to a Santander FinTech study, distributed ledger technology could reduce financial services infrastructure costs between US$15 billion and $20 billion per annum by 2022, providing the possibility to decommission legacy systems and infrastructure and significantly reduce IT costs. In response to these financial pressures, blockchain has already moved into this space. Startups are bringing new blockchain-model solutions promising efficiency; some companies are leaning into the immutable capabilities of blockchain—through Bitcoin—to pay employees with international employers; some are using blockchain encryption to validate college degrees during the recruitment process.

In a digital era, where trust is elusive and can be cost-intensive, blockchain's appeal will only continue to grow because, for those who take the time to understand its potential, it offers a clear way to confirm, validate, and authenticate values and events. And talent management may become the force ushering in some of the most significant and important forays into blockchain technologies: Market pundits are predicting that major firms will soon begin experimenting with blockchain solutions for this space, and many organizations already partner to shape blockchain's use in the talent sphere. The effects will be profound and pervasive, and I hope that the right people step up to the plate to oversee how blockchain networks are shaped and connected.

As you may already know, blockchain employs a distributed ledger system to securely transfer information and validate transactions through consensus. The best use for this technology is to disrupt slow, labor-intensive, and expensive processes. Processes that call for significant data collection or rely on third-party verification can be transformed. Blockchain will automatically settle disputes through historical records that are unalterable; likewise, candidates' employment history, accomplishments, skills, and education will be instantly accessible and immutable.

Already, some universities are exploring the possibility of an "educational passport," one element of what may, in the future, become our digital passports. The individuals themselves would maintain full ownership of their own data and decide who has access to it. No longer would they need to create a new resume for dozens of prospective employers. No more trying to squeeze twenty technology specialties or other skills onto a few pages of a PDF—all the information would be housed securely, validated, and available to anyone (and only those they choose).

Processes that present roadblocks will shift to smooth, streamlined exchanges of authenticated information that will be immediately available. Smart contracts delivered through blockchain will replace much of the onerous process of onboarding, especially for high-volume, high-turnover positions. When it comes to managing payroll or paying contract or temp workers, blockchain can dramatically reduce the hours required and increase efficiency while enhancing fraud prevention and easing the process of paying employees in other countries by removing the middleman in international payments. Employers would have access to a greater field of talent and the tools to help them identify and verify their next best hires.

The potential is hard to overstate.

All of this is not to say that we don't have work to do before we can achieve the kind of development and implementation to make blockchain work for us in the most uplifting, valuable ways possible. There is much work to be done and much to be considered. There are risks for early adopters, but there is also room for those early adopters to carve out a competitive advantage by choosing to lead rather than follow. My best advice for executives and others whose growth depends on people— which is to say *anyone*—is to begin the discovery journey *now*.

Elevating and Connecting

In my own personal journey, I've learned that when you're intentional about how you use technology and science, it's transformational.

The power of technology to transform lives has become increasingly clear. We now have the ability to connect to and harness the talent and potential of every human being, no matter where they sit—in a village in rural India, in sub-Saharan Africa, or in remote Appalachia.

Now, when I grew up in Bombay, contrasts surrounded us (just like in Manhattan today). Chinnu and Moni didn't shield us either. Especially not Chinnu, who had a very permeable and wide boundary of responsibility.

Awareness of the food insecurity that many faced was always in the periphery of our vision. In Bombay, there was both lack of access and spoilage in the tropical climates. The efforts of the government to distribute food and provide a social net of sorts were small steps dwarfed by the sheer volume of need and the scale of the country. People faced starvation due to poverty and also due to challenges in managing the supply and demand of food (among other issues).

When I was quite little, maybe six years old, I went to my parents' workplace. It is now a secure facility—no outsiders allowed—but back then, once a year, you could visit your parents at work. I remember gazing at the dome of Cirus.[9] I was fascinated, as I knew very few people were allowed to go inside.

More visible to me was my father's work on plants in labs and fields where they crisscrossed genes to develop sturdy strains that could produce more food. Teams also worked on the irradiation of food, which allows them to be stored for long periods of time. I saw plump chickpeas in a petri dish, side-by-side with their non-irradiated, shriveled brethren.

I was stunned. I remember thinking, "This is so amazing because this can prevent people from being hungry." Now, some of this insight may have been linked to the possibility of not having to "finish everything on the plate" anymore; but I also realized that, for the first time, that using technology with intention can create the kind of change that makes peoples' lives better.

If you put the human need at the heart of it all, it's very, very powerful.

When we think about what blockchain is really about, we need to focus on what it can solve. This technology is a connector. It holds enormous potential for solving supply and demand problems on so many levels, from food to careers. It can improve processes in financial transactions, as we've seen with cryptocurrency and Bitcoin already.

But what fascinated me, when I started thinking about how this can apply to talent and human transaction-related activities, is that it can link together to tap into the potential of people who are not part of the formal talent ecosystem.

Of course, a lot of our efforts in blockchain now are related to the formal economy, people who are in developed countries. Blockchain truly has the potential to be that connecting authenticator that can link people globally and provide a more level playing field and a platform where everybody can engage. That's not only irrespective of where they sit from a geopolitical or location perspective but also of where they live in socially constructed hierarchies. That's inspiring.

TWO

What Is Blockchain?

I'LL START by saying that I like the idea of blockchain technology. I'm inspired that it works through collaboration, coming together, solving problems, linking arms (and CPUs), with mutual validation.

Most of our conversation in this book focuses on the potential and the problems we can solve with blockchain, so in this chapter we'll spend some time discussing how blockchain technology works.

Technology is most interesting because of what it can do for us.

If you are flying somewhere, you probably don't worry (I hope) or think too much about how your airplane stays in the air. You might be mostly focused on that trip you're taking, the work you want to get done when you get there, or the holiday you'll have, now that we're back flying, post-pandemic. But knowing and being aware of the principles of lift, weight, thrust, and drag that keep the giant metal object in the air makes your journey a little more magical, wondrous.

Similarly, here, we'll briefly touch upon the principles of blockchain and how it works. But we'll mainly focus on the destination and how blockchain technology can help us experience the world, do business better, provide employment, connect people, and enable mobility.

So, where can the blockchain journey take us? What experiences can it transform? What problems can it solve?

We all know this, but it's worth repeating: The real force of any organization is the people who believe in it and spend every day making it better and stronger. The more people pull in the same direction, the greater the impact. The better and more aligned the talent and skills, the better the impact.

And, similarly, the impact of the global community, and our potential as the human race, is accelerated when we can tap into the potential everywhere, irrespective of the level in a social hierarchy or geographic location.

We know a fulfilling life on the individual level— one where people feel like they are empowered to grow and better themselves—can lead to an environment that is better for us all. As the individual pieces improve, so does the whole.

Coincidentally, this concept happens to be part of the underlying premise of blockchain. Each piece of the puzzle, fitting into the right position, makes all of us a little better off. But how do we take this technology and fit it into our own spaces? What's the real-world application for organizations, leaders, talent managers, or any member of the C-suite, particularly for something that seems to be much more the purview of IT departments? If it's well-planned and implemented, blockchain has the potential to improve every aspect of how we live, work, and do business.

Think about the way we exchange money today. We use it as a proxy for value: whatever you and I value. Much of it has shifted to happen online, with a series of trusted partners in the background —financial institutions acting as third parties— ensuring that your information is protected and verified and that the vendor receives payment.

Now let's say you value caffeine greatly, and when you need caffeine, you promise to pay for it with a credit card. The barista, assured that your credit card company will uphold the promise, dispenses four ounces of coffee and four ounces of foam. This is recorded as a transaction by your signature, or your app, which seals the deal with the barista. A few weeks later, your credit card bill presents that promise, which you fulfill by payment.

Even as you make a transaction in person, your information is shared across a network with many organizations who have a hand in making it happen. In this instance, Visa (or Mastercard) uses your credit score as the estimate of your credibility and intent to pay. This credit score from Experian

or Equifax or TransUnion (in the United States) is issued based on data provided by other third parties. These third parties that provide input on your regularity in paying your bills may vary, from your mortgage holder, your car company, Home Depot or Macy's (where, in a misguided effort to make the most of a Labor Day Sale, you may have signed up for a credit card), and your dentist. All these data sets together present a picture of your creditworthiness. The credit bureau is entirely reliant on the data provided by this random assortment of people and organizations.

This network of trust verification allows you to get your caffeine fix on a promise that they under-write. Without verified, trusted third parties, there is no means to make cashless payments or get your coffee through a communication network.

Any mistake, by any link in this motley network, can impact lives. And mistakes are common. Anyone who has had to dispute a credit card transaction or correct a mistake on their credit report unearthed while applying for a mortgage knows the pain and the likelihood of this. If you are a CFO (or hoping to become one), a bad credit score can impact your chances of holding an executive job. Apart from mistakes, fraud happens. There are information breaches, and purchasers still sometimes get away with using stolen payment information. Right now, commerce happens almost exclusively through this inherently flawed system, a trust-based model.

If the payment you made to the barista was irreversible and unchangeable, or "immutable," we wouldn't need the slew of third parties. An immutable payment record would guarantee the barista security of payment, with no need for an intermediary.

But in the absence of confident verification of your ability to purchase, transactions need to be backed by proof that you can pay, each time. Someone or something (the verifying agency, or the credit card company in this case) provides that proof. That increases transaction costs, which means small, casual transactions aren't worth providing, which creates an opportunity loss. Nonreversible payments for nonreversible services can't happen, and vendors have to gather more information than they might otherwise need. It's inefficient and it closes the door to speedy, small payments.

The trouble with trust, in this sense, is that it can't scale in a reliable way. It's also difficult to scale it on a global level.

Years ago, when I landed on the shores of California, it was impossible to find a financial institution that would underwrite my coffee. No one believed that I would pay them back. There was no guarantee or trust in my ability to pay; it was impossible to get a credit card or process a transaction

LIZEBETH VARGHESE

without cash. I had a pretty good job, a master's degree, a valid visa, a bank account in the Bayview Savings Bank. I also had decent skills, money in my pocket, but no financial trust. I was basically unbanked and unable to access the cashless economy. It was impossible to be issued a credit card, with no US credit history, because **I had no "provenance."**

There are millions in a similar situation—without the ability to bank, access the cashless economy, or tap into the virtual economy—within the societies in which they grew up and live (not just in the societies into which they travel).

An electronic payment system built on cryptographic proof would change all this, allowing parties to skip the middlemen. The barista could be protected from fraud because payments would be nonreversible; the caffeine seeker wouldn't have to re-share a wealth of sensitive information every time they need to make a purchase.

Similarly, when we try to hire somebody, we need to know if their antecedents are correct. Did they really go to the school they claim? Do they have the skills they tout? Were they employed at the companies on record? For how long? Each time we need to understand these antecedents, we exchange information back and forth, accepting the credibility of some third parties and not of others. The third parties are not infallible, and errors are rampant. Anyone who has tried to get their credit history corrected or, worse, has had their identity stolen, has struggled with the errors made by validators.

So how do we create that cryptographic proof? How can we build trust? How can blockchain do this for us?

The rather mysterious Satoshi Nakamoto popularized Blockchain technology. No one really knows if Nakamoto is a real person, or multiple people, male or female. In fact, the abstract of Nakamoto's article actually uses the pronoun "we." Perhaps like Shakespeare, Nakamoto may be a woman. There is a lot you can look up on the internet about the myth and conjecture that abounds about Nakamoto's identity: Nakamoto lived here, was spotted there, paid for this in Bitcoin, and so on.

What we do know is that—in 2008, Satoshi Nakamoto and Martti Malmi created a website called "Bitcoin.org." Later that year, Nakamoto published a paper on this site called "Bitcoin: A Peer-to-Peer Electronic Cash System," which described a protocol to achieve tamper-proof, decentralized verification of transactions, prevent double-spending and generate a transparent record in payments. Nakamoto's paper[1] built on prior work on immutable and irrefutable linked timestamp and hashes by Stornetta and Haber,[2] Ricardian contracts by Ian Grigg[3] and work on keys for crypto systems by Ralph Merkle.[4]

Nakamoto identified and solved the following three key barriers to trust in transactions:

1. Provenance: Trusting the source and history leading up to a particular moment, the antecedents of a transaction. Or as my Ammachi might have asked: "Who is the potential groom? Was he ever married before? How far back does the family go?"

2. Immutability: Trusting the validity and proof of information, having absolute certainty that the transaction is what it purports to be. "Do we know these facts about the groom's salary for sure? What is the proof?"

3. Decentralization: Validity that comes from multiple verifiers and authenticators. Democratization of affirmation from everyone who is allowed to participate in the network, not just from centralized arbiters of truth. "Does everyone (of relevance) know that they are married? Does everyone agree?" In my view, this is the principle underlying the hitherto inexplicable Indian custom of inviting everyone you know to a wedding.

Blockchain technology operates on the principle of a shared, validated ledger. A ledger is a record of information, like a journal. A distributed ledger is a record of information that others can view, like your bank statement. You can choose who can see the ledger. Access is authorized and time-stamped by technology which eliminates the need for third-party validation or any unique certifying authority who needs to validate every transaction to confirm its provenance.

Blockchain, an immutable, digital distributed ledger, records and distributes the history of transactions between parties. By using timestamps that record each transaction, the ledger creates a sequence of transactions, into a chain—the blockchain—encrypted by a key. The transactions are recorded on multiple ledgers that participate, each keeping an identical copy. As a result, the verifying authority is not a centralized body, a single keeper of the truth. Instead, the validation is democratized: Every ledger contributes to the verification process.

I'll touch upon a few features of blockchain technology because I refer to them later in the book.

A LEGO block works well to visualize how blockchain works. All LEGO blocks have connectors—the cylindrical pegs that allow connection to each other. There are rules (of how the blocks need to be placed) to abide by if you want to connect. The blocks append to each other in sequence and build on each other (based on rules or a smart contract).

The basic component block has two parts:

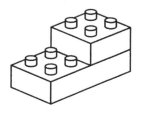

1. The main block holds all the information about the transaction and all the

transactions that happened at the same instant. It also uses a hash algorithm and encryption to prevent tampering with the data and uniquely identifies the block. This gives each block a fingerprint, tied to its very existence. And, like a fingerprint or iris scan tied to a person's genetic makeup, erasure or tampering with the fingerprint invalidates the block.

2. A metadata layer (like the pegs) holds information to connect to the chain. It stores information about the block it was connected to before (its parent block) as well as data to allow connection to the next block. In addition, there is the timestamp, which records when the block was created (linking to its authentication), and also the prior timestamp, to build the sequentially linked chain. There are other attributes like the poetically named Merkle tree[5] (named for Ralph Merkle), child nodes, leaf nodes, and more, which I won't discuss here. All these pieces of metadata help preserve integrity and provide provenance of the transaction.

The proof of a transaction is based on the degree of universality of consensus and when the majority of the blocks affirm the data. This democratization of validation means that a centralized verifier is not required. Any transaction is broadcast to the whole network, and everyone maintains the same record. Even if a node or participant leaves, they can return and accept the longest chain. This is, in effect, the distributed ledger principle that underlies blockchain.

The ledger is the recorded history of exchanges of goods and services between two individuals. A distributed ledger is a recorded history of exchanges between multiple parties that can be reviewed and accessed (but not changed) by everyone in that network.

A blockchain is a digital distributed ledger. Different terms used to describe how blockchain is deployed—permissionless, permissioned, public and private. Public blockchains are those where anyone can join, and participate. The most famous blockchain projects of Bitcoin and Ethereum are public and permissionless, and are said to have risen as a response to the financial crisis of 2008. Anyone can join these blockchains, create an address without sharing any personal information, and interact with anonymity. The ability to edit the rules, make changes or control the flow of information doesn't reside in the hands of any one individual or entity. All transactions are visible, with full decentralization and validation by each node. All changes need to be adopted and agreed upon by at least half of the nodes or users—the "majority consensus protocol." The effort to validate a transaction is the "Proof of Work" ("Proof of Stake" in Ethereum) that "miners" in a blockchain perform. The miners spend time and computing power to validate and broadcast a transaction within the network. Most permissionless blockchains use some mechanism (like tokens) to incentivize users. The discussions we frequently encounter on the cost of computation of blockchain are based on the energy and computational power needed to validate each transaction in a permissionless blockchain.

Blockchains can also be private, where participation is restricted to known, selected participants who form consortiums for a reason, to exchange information and complete transactions based on agreed-upon consensus mechanisms. Permissioned blockchains[6] have restricted participation, and need permission or agreement from other participants or a governing body. These permissions can be customized to needs, with appropriate protections for privacy. Only those who need to know certain pieces of information will have access, depending on the setup and parameters you establish with others in the blockchain. These permissioned blockchains can be fully or partially decentralized as needed and choose their methods of consensus. The Hyperledger Fabric[7] is an example of a permissioned blockchain platform which is built on Linux open-source..

We see the increasing adoption of blockchain in the financial sector (with permissioned blockchains like Corda[8] and Quorum[9]) because information is safer by creating automated trust and that all-important immutability:

- An append-only historic version of the truth
- An inherent ability to detect tampering
- Increased transparency for permissioned participants, including regulators

That append-only element creates certainty. Additions can be made through what we call nodes, which provide a unique method of allowing information to be added without corrupting the existing, validated information. These nodes can be added or removed from the network without consequence. No node is responsible for the database as a whole, and nodes can easily catch up if they've been removed and then come back online. This process simplifies disaster recovery processes, as there is no need to manage multiple databases.

It also creates opportunities for process optimization by significantly reducing or eliminating reconciliation costs and automating business processes via smart contracts. Cost savings arise by decommissioning expensive processes to manage and secure central databases. Instead, you increase transparency by decentralizing, because external parties and regulators can immediately access the ledger. Across the board, you can identify opportunities to reduce errors, latency, risk, cost, and capital requirements—and those benefits can be easily extended to new members without significant integration costs. Think of software upgrades that don't require endless migration time, effort, and money.

This doesn't mean that blockchain is infallible, because if the transaction data is incorrect to begin with, it perpetuates and immortalizes the error until a new transaction block is added to correct it. But once the data is verified, it can be used to validate, streamline, and enable the exchange of information and value (like caffeine in our example).

While the idea of sharing or distributing information more widely may make some of us feel uncertain, the distributed ledger is not new at all.

Every day, we constantly distribute copies of our information to networks: to the barista when we swipe our credit card, to a company server when we send an email, and to others when we cc them. Even when we send a group text to family and friends, we actually create a shared record of our conversation. And in all of these transactions and communications, there is a historical record.

In the words of F. Scott Fitzgerald, "The test of a first-rate intelligence is the ability to hold two opposed ideas in the mind at the same time, and still retain the ability to function." This quote sums up the dichotomy of blockchain—it is the balance of trust-less proof based on the algorithm, married with consensus through democratized validation from all the participants or nodes.

The Current and Future Blockchain

Blockchain, uses distributed ledger technology to quickly verify exchanges and prevents historical records from being modified. It offers a number of solutions to ongoing challenges within talent management. There are some barriers, however, including the fact that multiple parties need to adopt the technology for it to live up to that potential. It's a lot like the early days of the internet. Some people had access; others didn't. It existed more in clusters and smaller networks. Who could have imagined how ubiquitous it would become?

Initially, "the blockchain" is a series of different blockchains or networks, which can operate together. In the early days of the internet, it was a small network of people who trusted each other. And it was a safe space where information was exchanged. As more and more of those networks connected, it became much larger in value and types of transactions. Now we have the World Wide Web.

Blockchain is already moving in a similar direction.

The criteria for whether or not blockchain is the right solution revolves around the quality of the data, the amount available, and how immutable it needs to be.

We can start with the basics. Increasingly in the world of business (and healthcare and academia and…err…Netflix), you and I deal with large amounts of sensitive data. Personal data. The ability to access information on an as-needed basis is imperative, as is the ability to ensure compliance with federal laws. These challenges provide the opportunity for a blockchain solution.

You may be squeamish about this or hesitant to adopt something that feels so sprawling, without a means of direct control by individuals. There are risks and concerns to be addressed, as there are with any new technology. In my mind—and for many other experts—this is less a question of whether blockchain will become part of HR operations and more a question of when. Blockchain is going to be an inevitable technology in which we capture and share information on talent and in business. Those of us who learn its potential benefits early on will be better positioned to embrace them.

One of the key requirements is groups of people and organizations that trust each other forming consortiums with mutually agreed-upon rules.

But the current use of these consortiums of trust are, so far, small. Eventually, when more and more users and organizations sign on to consortiums to share information, we will be able to navigate a worldwide web of talent—the Universal Talent Exchange, which we'll cover soon—in a safer, easier way.

This, again, mimics where we were with the internet. When I was in school in India, we had mostly intranets, to communicate within the organization.

And those were secure intranets because they were securely closed, easily manageable environments. We dialed up and out to connect to the internet and the world outside and did not share much personal information. The magic of the World Wide Web materialized when all these groups of intranets started trusting each other and connecting with each other. We agreed on some protocols to share information and set up safety protocols to the point that I now feel comfortable putting my credit card information online to buy something from somebody in Europe or somebody in India. What changed? We agreed on rules of engagement or trust that people believed in and agreed upon.

The use of blockchain is, in many ways, not very different, except that it's much more secure. It won't require my transaction to go to my bank or high school for authentication because those networks of trust will already be established. And information will be accessible. It will become a passport where you can immediately share or submit information that is verified and cannot be stolen or altered. You can trust that what I'm showing you is accurate because that's what blockchain does: enables that trusted transaction with ease without having to get third parties involved.

Once adoption becomes prevalent, think about the implications: an easy, simple, trusted flow of information among high schools and higher educational institutions, financial institutions, medical institutions, hospitals, private practices, and the legal system. Think of all the trouble right now that can come with simply gathering verified information across state lines in the United States. Blockchain is so much bigger than that. It's a global solution that I believe will become ubiquitous, which is when and where its power lies. It's coming whether we like it or not and whether we're ready or not.

I'm among those who would prefer to be ready.

It will likely change how you perform your job—for the better—and transform what you can do. More than ever before, organizations realize that as technology becomes more accessible, people make the difference. And competitive advantage comes from providing aspiration, access, and opportunities. The democratization of opportunity is going to be pivotal and critical.

Blockchain can make several standard talent processes quicker, which creates a more positive employee experience and, ultimately, value. Here's how blockchain can make the important work you do even better:

Transparency and Audibility (Provenance)

As businesses increasingly move toward Software as a Service (SaaS) platforms to move data to the efficient and cost-effective cloud, the need for transparency and trust in data becomes all the more important.

Privacy

Employee data contains personal information, as we all know very well. Business and HR clients need to be sure that data cannot be compromised and is only viewed on a need-to-know basis.

Trustworthiness and Efficiency

Organizations need to adhere to all government regulations related to employee data, oftentimes in several different countries that may or may not vary in requirements. They also need to adapt to changes in the laws, the more nimble and quicker moving, the better.

Think for a moment about the way we do things now. How do we move data around? How about when we need to update technology? Remember the last time your organization performed a major tech upgrade? Things can go wrong. Time is almost always lost. Everyone has to re-learn where and how to find the information they need. It can be frustrating for everyone involved to make those kinds of changes.

Imagine the efficiency and cost savings of a well-built blockchain when it solves the following:

Business Function	How Transactions Currently Occur (Without Blockchain)	Business Impact
Transferring data between two parties	Data transfer process includes converting from one format to another	Time and resources are used
Storing similar data on multiple systems	Limited governance exists to define and enforce data quality	Data can contradict each other Cleaning data for regulators is time intensive
Old technology	Batch feeds, or breaking up big data into smaller chunks (batches), are used to fetch data Unstructured data, such as digital copies of documents, is still manually sifted through	Data retrieval is not instantaneous, costing time

The element of immutability is what possibly holds the most promise for the field of human resources. A distributed ledger offers instant verification of client credentials and identity, and it keeps a verified historical record of past transactions. Once data has been written, no one—not even a system administrator—can change it. This is relevant to the entire chain of interactions a human resources executive or manager might have with employees, beginning with recruitment or earlier with an applicant's previous training and education. Schools, previous employers, and government agencies have a copy of the applicant's resume and personal information, thus verifying its authenticity. Human resources has a copy of the applicant's data, including a historical copy of any changes going as far back as the history of the chain.

Institutions verify any changes that the candidate makes to a resume or personal information before it is shared with everyone with a copy of the ledger. When it's time to sit down with the applicant for a discussion, the interviewer can then accurately rely on the resume's content. The same process applies during an employee's entire tenure with the company: when they request a move to a different division, update personal information, add accomplishments or training, or make any pertinent change. Block by block, the individual and the organization are adding to the chain. Add thousands upon thousands of participating organizations, the future of the blockchain, and you have a reliable, verified whole—a full circle network that makes each link in the chain that much stronger.

THREE

The Universal Talent Exchange

FINDING the right person for the job is an old, old story. And the journeys to make those connections are often long stories.

When we lived in small communities, everyone knew who to turn to for the expertise they needed, whether a doctor, a craftsman, or an expert in any other trade or profession. Those experts were also neighbors, people they had known all their lives. As communities grew, and as we became more mobile and our networks expanded, we needed a way to prove our expertise to new groups and those farther from our home.

Carpenters, also known as journeymen, offered an innovative solution to this. They would travel from town to town, offering their services. As they did so, they began carrying a traveling book to collect stamps from other artisans they worked with along the way as evidence of their skills and experience.

These books were how individuals could trust the journeyman to do work for them.

The journeyman was responsible for tracking his credentials via his physical log of experience, which came to be called a "wanderbuch." These traveling books fit the bill, for a time, and at least gave clients a sense of who they were hiring and whether they could trust them to do the job well.

Of course, the world has changed just a little bit since then.

"YOU'RE TOO LATE. The exam started twenty minutes ago," the proctor said.

"But I've come from so far away," Atul pleaded, his voice shaking a bit. "This is my one chance. Please. I'm Atul Jagat. Applicant number 2275. I have all my paperwork here."

He was embarrassed as he saw people raise their heads from their papers. But everyone quickly looked away and continued to write. Every minute counted. With thousands of applicants competing for thirty seats, everyone needed high scores to get to the next round.

Atul was so ready to take this exam. This morning, everything seemed possible. What if he passed the exam? What if he got into this master's program? He would have a degree from this amazing institute. He would have proof that he was talented. The world would have evidence that everything he had worked for was real. He would be the right person for so many job opportunities. No one else in his family would have to study under the light of a neighbor's outdoor lamp. No one else would have to work in the sugar-cane farms. His heart sinking, Atul felt everything slip away.

∾

THE WANDERBUCHS BECAME RESUMES—a tidy page or two, typed up, that clearly laid out background, skills, certifications, and the like.

But today, of course, hiring managers don't just peruse a few slips of paper anymore. Maybe that was the case twenty-five or thirty years ago. Long gone are the days when a handful of people mailed in resumes in response to a job posting in a newspaper. Today's talent executives manage people and systems that sort through digital resumes that would fill an entire room, often to fill a single position. Today, the world is at their fingertips.

Those small groups and intimate communities with the occasional traveling workers, doctors, or priests have converged into a landscape that liter-ally spans the globe.

To understand the breadth of the opportunity, we need to zoom out again—from small communities to connected continents—and shift our perspective from the place and culture we know best. The group of people we're talking about varies greatly depending on the lens you use. So, if you look at it from a North American lens, it's one kind of market, with its own nuances, trends, and variations. If you look at it from a worldwide lens, the picture changes dramatically.

Let's start with the global market.

When you consider how many people may be vying for jobs, or at least available for jobs, on a global scale, what number do you think of? Millions of professionals around the world? Who do you picture? People in suits, right? You picture people the way they look when they show up for a job interview at an office.

What the global market of talent really represents is something different. Every person has talent. This isn't just executives or high-level professionals or people in developed countries we're talking about.

Think of all the people on our planet, about 7.9 billion,[1] expected to reach 8 billion in 2023. That really is our talent ecosystem, because each of those 7.9 billion is a person who has skills to contribute in some way. Now, the truth is that only about 60 percent of the world's population are formally employed. But many others make their living in the informal economy.

Agriculture. Beekeeping. Foraging. Sugarcane pressing. Cotton farming. Manual scavenging. All professions that represent how people earn their livelihood. We often forget what life is like outside our office complexes or corporate campuses. Let's take in the vast population across the globe. Remember that the human race is not encompassed in North America or in developed countries but includes developing and underdeveloped countries. In the small mofussil towns, in the remote villages, there are entire populations of skills and exceptional talent waiting to be discovered. Like my friend Atul.

That's the good news; it's also part of our biggest challenge.

$\sim$

THAT FEBRUARY MORNING, when Atul walked through the gates of the Borivali railway station, he wasn't exactly sure where to go or how to buy a ticket. So, he inserted himself into the crowd of people moving forward, en masse, into the enclosure. He held his friend Veer's elbow gently, guiding him into the flow as Veer's white cane was redundant in this current of humanity. Atul was a bit nervous to be in Bombay for the first time, but being part of this purposeful swarm of buzzing men and women gave him a thrill of achievement. He was here.

Atul had never imagined being able to take this exam for this master's program. It was unaffordable. The expense was not an adequate reason to sell the goat and sheep, which represented their family's emergency fund. The exam location was too far, Bombay too expensive to travel to, and his chance to land one of the thirty seats too small. So when Veer was invited to a conference for the blind, he encouraged Atul to accompany him as Veer's "sighted companion." Atul could travel for free and then use the opportunity to take the exam. And so here they were.

AND THAT'S why blockchain is so important and helpful because blockchain can provide a way for us to actually tap into this entire population of skills, both formal and informal. It has the ability to identify, validate, and provide a platform for people of different skills in different locations to engage and participate in work. Employers broaden their pool of talent to find more of the skills they need, and steady, stable employment becomes more accessible.

How vast is that untapped talent pool? In Africa, about 86 percent of employment is informal; in Asia, it's 68 percent.[2] Right there, those are millions of people left out of the equation, partially because of education, partially because they don't have access to formal sector jobs. So if the people in sub-Saharan Africa who may be foraging right now, living in poverty, were given the training to code—if they were able to write code, if they were able to participate—how much more effective would we be as a global community?

The current state of the talent market is facing intense disruption. Businesses are changing very rapidly. The rate of change is faster than we've ever seen before, too. Things are not only changing, they're changing more frequently and more dramatically, and what happens to any company is going to happen faster. Think of Amazon. They started out as a bookseller. Now, they're also a space exploration company. Same thing with the record label—Virgin Records, reborn as Virgin Galactic. And of course, Tesla, the car company for early adopters turned into a leader in the final frontier. All of these companies compete and collaborate with NASA and other space agencies while spawning an ecosystem of smaller companies who follow their lead. The barrier of entry to entering every industry, even the most inaccessible one of space exploration has dropped, so all kinds of players enter, disrupting business models rapidly. Car companies were disrupted by Uber. Hotel companies were disrupted by Airbnb. The quality of teaching in schools is challenged and disrupted by the Khan Academy. The list goes on and on, across the spectrum.

That ongoing business disruption requires a very different kind of talent. The needs of each business are constantly changing, so this demand for talent is also very dynamic. Along with that, the skills that are needed are evolving and emerging all the time. New skills are going to be required daily because new technologies are being developed and refined—from quantum computing to geo satellites, which are becoming mainstream. Not only is the talent market actually much larger than we think, it's also much more dynamic and complex than we think. And it's not fully responsive to what we actually need because the pace of change and skill requirements are much faster than the acquisition of skills. Despite that huge number we started with—six billion—we still don't have enough people with the right skills. Imagine if there was a way to solve that dilemma. Companies could grow, more people could reach their potential and take better care of themselves and their families, and we could raise the standard of living across the globe.

∾

ATUL AND VEER had come from their village on the outskirts of Nagpur, in the interior of Maharashtra. Atul figured that since he had got them this far, he could guide them across the rest. Their plan was to take the local train that went east, across the city, then south, to reach Dadar and then take the Number 8 bus to their destination. The exam began at noon, and he had plenty of time. Or that's what Atul thought

That February morning, moved along by the deluge of people, Atul and Veer found themselves on the railway platform. They still needed to buy their tickets. They had one hundred rupees to cover all their expenses for the day. Unsure of where to go, they approached the only official-looking person in sight—the ticket checker (TC).

"Sir, where can we buy a ticket?" Atul asked.

"What do you mean where can you buy a ticket? If you don't have a ticket, you shouldn't be here on the platform. Show me your ticket. I am the ticket checker! You dare ask me?" he thundered officiously.

"But we don't know where to buy the ticket, which is why we are asking you. We came to you thinking you could help us."

Managing the Deluge

I often work with C-suite leaders on their strategy initiatives as they try to transform their organizations. The truth is that whether it's a chief marketing officer trying to shift the customer experience, a CIO trying to rationalize the IT application portfolio, a CEO seeking to modernize the mainframe the company runs on, or a board trying to make their culture more inclusive, it all boils down to whether there is clarity on the new work that needs to be done. Equally important is whether there is clarity on the availability of skills and experiences to do things differently.

Strategy is meaningless unless we are able to decode it into the basic building blocks, the LEGO blocks of skills. A lot of the work done by external strategists falls flat for this reason—it doesn't take it all the way through into actionable realities for the people who have to do the work.

~

THE TC SHRUGGED IRRITABLY. "All I know is that if you are on the platform without a ticket, you need to pay a fine. There is a hundred rupee fine for cheats."

"A fine?" Atul's heart sank. Veer started tapping his cane on the ground nervously.

But we didn't do anything wrong. We don't have a lot of money, sir. We've only a hundred rupees between us."

"Tell me, are you on the platform?"

"Yes sir, we are."

"Do you have tickets?"

"No, sir, we don't."

"Then pay the fine."

Finally, daunted by curious onlookers who gathered and seeing the Veer's conference agenda and the emptied-out pockets of the two men, the TC relented. A little bit.

"Give me fifty rupees, and I'll give you two tickets. I don't have any change. Your tickets cost forty. Ten rupees is your fine for wasting my time."

Rattled but relieved; Atul and Veer hurried away to board the train to Dadar, the next step of their journey.

THE TRUTH IS, work has become more complex. Knowledge work, in every domain, requires a multidisciplinary approach. It is for this reason of complexity that the disaggregation of work into component skills becomes important.[3] Hiring based on skills is 5x more predictive of future performance than hiring for education and 2.5x more predictive than hiring for work experience. Hiring for skills decreases time-to-hire and diversifies candidate pools.[4] And, hiring for skills increases retention.[5]

In my conversations and work with CEOs on talent strategy, we often focus on skills as the building block, the most basic element of a job and key to implementing strategy. I like to use the analogy of a LEGO block for a skill because as jobs and strategies become more complex, they all comprise a string or stack of LEGO blocks that need to make the whole. And, just like there are creative maps that can help you make aircraft carriers and cities out of LEGO blocks, if you have the right skill blocks put together in the right combination, you can create or transform anything.

For example, my work in the space of talent has become increasingly layered. When I received my master's in management (from the Tata Institute of Social Sciences, back in Mumbai) in the mid-1990s, we took psychology, organization theory, economics, statistics, marketing, labor relations, and talent processes, among other things. As I started to work, this education stood me in good stead. But over the years, we started to see the infusion of technology into our work, "e-HR" or electronically enabled HR processes! The rise of technology in our world has moved along to require understanding of technology, portals, employee experience, social media, content curation, online communities, robotic process automation, integration with other HR systems, and the enablement of process flows with technology.

And just as a C-suite leader needs to understand this for the organizations at large, managers need to have this understanding at any level of operation. We must be able to describe and document it in a way that allows for common understanding with the people and teams we work with. In order to do work completely and fruitfully, we need to be able to describe a job or a task in a language and words that reflect the common understanding of the people we work with. In most organizations this effort is like the Tower of Babel where different words are used to describe this increasing complexity of skills and degree of expertise.

AFTER GETTING off the train at Dadar, Atul and Veer waited at the bus stop for the Number 8 bus that would take them to their destination. Kirandeep Singh was waiting there as usual, watching for train passengers who could be a long-distance fare to the outer suburbs. He dismissed the two who were clearly not able to afford his taxi fare. But as he waited, Kiran amused himself by watching the duo pace at the bus stop, yet not board any bus. After observing them for a while, he walked up to them.

"Tusīṁ itzār ki kara rahē hō [Why are you waiting]?"
"We're waiting for the Number 8 bus to go to Deonar. I'm going to be late for the exam! When will the bus come? Do you know?" Atul gazed with interest at the tall, turbaned, and bearded man. He hadn't ever met or spoken to a Punjabi Sikh; he'd only ever seen them in Bollywood movies.

Kiran nodded. "So, what's your friend doing? Is he going to take the exam too?" Veer jumped in to explain the whole story. Kiran looked at Atul and Veer closely, "Theek hain [okay]. Tell me exactly where you want to go."

Atul pulled out his exam ticket and pointed to the address. Kiran sighed. "You want to get all the way there? You're at the wrong bus stop. You need to go left, then right, over the bridge to catch the Number 8. Use the footbridge to cross over to the traffic heading north. It's about a twenty-minute walk to the correct stop."

"Walk twenty minutes?" Atul gulped, looking at Veer's cane.

AS WE DISCUSSED in the previous chapter, if we continue with the analogy of a LEGO block for a skill—jobs and strategies become more complex—they all comprise a string or stack of LEGO blocks that need to make the whole. This also implies that as jobs and work become more complex, we need to disaggregate the skills needed into layers and differences to understand them and do them well. And we need to find a way to understand the best way in which skills can be acquired or accessed to complete complex tasks.

If we are able to parse strategy into its component LEGO blocks, we can also find the best talent to work on that particular component. And if we can find the best talent irrespective of where they sit, we get to a much better outcome. So, how can we do that?

There is a hilarious standup bit, "In Britain, we process happiness differently," by British comedian Bill Bailey. Bill talks through the differences between Australians' intense, aggressively enthusiastic greetings and the British standard response to almost any inquiry involving the state of their well-being: "Not too bad."

While the delivery is less than enthusiastic, he dives into what he calls the "ludicrous optimism" of British society (as demonstrated by Britain having the highest percentage of convertible vehicles in Europe). That, he insists, is "preposterous optimism."

This generational trait sometimes comes along with an additional phrase, especially when some time has passed between meetings: "Not too bad, all things considered." At this, he's awestruck. He is shouting at this point: "I want to say to them, 'You have considered all things?'" Then he launches into a long, rapid-fire list of the truly astounding items to consider in the universe, including the "baffling longevity of LinkedIn." He pauses at that one; it gets quite a laugh from the audience.

That tidbit lands somewhere between other astounding things to consider—wars, religion, ideology, and the uncountable stars. Why is it such a zinger? What made LinkedIn so ubiquitous, and what can its longevity, twenty years and counting, tell us about the global talent market?

It demonstrates that there is a need for a global platform for talent and opportunities and that the need isn't going anywhere. Like the patterns of change we see in industry disruption, it's growing at a faster rate than ever. Of course, it also has its shortcomings: Passive talent that may be the all-star you need for your position may not be using LinkedIn (or checking their messages), which limits the entire pool. It's also much more likely to be used in developed countries, and it is, like a resume, reliant on user-provided information. You can fake much on your profile and even game the social media-style algorithm in your favor.

Beyond LinkedIn, there are search engine-based models where many recruiters are finding talent: Think of the Indeeds and the Monster.coms of the world. Like the wanderbuchs, they arose in response to a pressing need. They work well on some levels, but they fail to respond to a couple of major challenges. The first is that it's not the volume of potential talent that is typically the core issue, as we've mentioned. Depending on the job type, it may be easy for recruiters to find somebody in a particular skill set. The question is, are they the best resource for that job? Are they the exact right fit?

It's not just about finding a warm body to do something. It's finding the best person for the job, at the right time.

VEER BLURTED OUT, upset. "How are we going to find the bus stop, Atul? We're already so late...all this effort...." Then Veer rallied, "We'll ask someone if we get lost. Come on, Atul, you are going to ace the exam."

Kiran sighed and interjected, "You know, I can drop you."

Atul replied quickly. "Sorry, we have no money. We can't afford your fare."

Kiran smiled at him and lied, "Don't worry, I was going there anyway to get my lunch. Let's go. I can get you to the bus stop in five minutes."

Atul helped Veer into the taxi and adjusted his cane. They sat back anxiously and gratefully as Kiran wiped his windshield with a dirty yellow duster and put his Fiat in gear.

Atul sat back, realizing that he was in a taxi for the very first time in his life. As he watched Kiran skillfully maneuver through the crowds of people and stray cows, he held the strap firmly and felt his throat tighten with emotion.

He remembered his Aai [mother] saying sadly, "Atul, you cannot study late. We can't afford to keep the electric light on for you. Study during the day."

Atul had watched his parents work in the sugarcane fields and knew the full worth of the toil that went into every single rupee. But he needed to study for his high school certificate exams run by the state government. Kids all over the state took the same exam; and if he did well, there would be scholarships for college. Atul read of kids who studied under street lights in Bombay and was envious. It was 1990, but their village had no streetlights for him to use.

BEYOND THAT IS the demand issue. Everybody will suddenly want the same kind of talent for certain rapidly emerging opportunities. So, the most expert talent—your most digitally savvy talent—is wanted by every company at the same time. Despite the availability of accessible global platforms to network, they become very scarce.

What happens then? The talent market shifts into a buyer's market for that segment of skills. Companies that want to move forward, companies whose trajectories depend in large part on finding the perfect fit when it comes to talent (which is to say, any growing company), what they really need to do is define communities. They need to find new ways to attract or develop talent from these networks.

That's why we see recruiters active in these networks of certain skill groups. Nurses have these virtual watering holes where they get together, and they are looking for jobs where they interact, where there are others like them, and where there is a sense of trust. There are different communities where nurses (and savvy recruiters) connect. That's one way to make progress. It, of course, has limitations.

Similarly, with the recognition of the value of parsing jobs into skills, we are able to access a much broader pool of talent. One example is the benefits of tapping into the potential of talent that is not neurotypical. Many folks who are neuro-atypical may have skills that allow them to be exceptionally creative—detail oriented or able to work with numbers—even if they may not have skills that help them navigate a regular interview process. People like Da Vinci, Carl Jung, and Winston Churchill are examples of people who are supposed to have been dyslexic along with those like Whoopi Goldberg, Steven Spielberg, and Tom Cruise. Increasingly, organizations understand how to uncover and leverage the abilities of folk whose skills may not be measurable through a typical rubric. SAP, Microsoft, EY, JP Morgan, and other companies have hiring and development programs that tap into atypical talent pools.

This is also the case of quantity versus quality—and, importantly, distinguishing and verifying the quality from the vast, global quantity. Because technology is so ubiquitous, and as more and more people have access to it, you'd think it would be easier to find good talent. Finding good talent, surprisingly, is actually becoming harder.

As with companies entering the market, the barrier of entry has dropped for candidates, too. That's simply because entry is a possibility, whether you're qualified or not. It's kind of like higher education applications. Even if you don't have a good LSAT score, if it's easy enough, you will still apply to Harvard, because you think, *Well, why not?* This is both a good thing and a bad thing for recruiters.

It increases the volume of applicants exactly the way it does in college applications. That's challenging because then you actually have to read through all of them. You have to sift through them, process information, and make sure you're not making biased or prejudiced decisions. You are, after all, making life-changing decisions. This affects livelihoods. It can affect entire generations of people.

AAI ENCOURAGED him to study and pushed him to read more. But Atul didn't know where to find more books. Atul's brain raced ahead in Marathi, and he painted his dilemmas in poignant poetry. But English escaped him. It was hard to improve his English without opportunities to read beyond the primer or speak with anyone. So Atul asked his neighbors for books, anything he could lay his hands

upon. But books were scarce, not something people bought or owned.

One of their neighbors who they called Baiji [respected grandmother] said she could lend one book owned by her late husband. "Read it. He was very fond of this book."

Atul demurred. "It's in English and complicated."

"So what if you cannot understand philosophy? Try to read it. You will learn something from it." Baiji looked approvingly at Atul's earnest face. "You know, because I'm old, I go to bed early. But I always leave the light above my front door on, even after I go to bed. You can come sit outside my front door and study if you like. It doesn't matter where you study or what you read, as long as you learn, right?"

THE PANDEMIC HAS SHOWN us that the democratization of skills and work is real, and we need to embrace it. Kids can study from home (it's difficult and not ideal but possible as home-schoolers know). People can work from home. **Skills don't reduce or degrade by distance.**

Ambition is not a function of location. And, if you can provide flexibility, remote work, and secure access, the world is your talent source.

Many companies have seen this during the pandemic. People moved to the locations where they wanted to be. I'm sure all of us know people who worked from their parent's home (in Falls Church, Virginia, or Mumbai, India), their vacation home in Puerto Rico, or the great summer dream: the RV on the road. We may still want some people to co-locate or be in a certain place, but we don't necessarily need that all the time anymore.

We're also seeing the rise of gig work. Of the US adult workforce, approximately 36 percent are gig workers, contributing to 5.7 percent of our GDP. Estimates show this rising to 52 percent in the next couple of years. In countries with younger populations, people lean more toward flexible and non-traditional work, and in countries like India and Mexico, 97 percent of people are open to alternate work models. When FreshBooks surveyed gig workers, 65 percent of them reported that "controlling their own career" means "freedom to choose when to work" and 56 percent said that it's "freedom to choose how hard to work." In the same survey, 48 percent of respondents said they favor freelancing because of the autonomy in managing career development, while 31 percent chose that type of working relationship simply because they don't like reporting to others. This is a real shift that is only going to accelerate.

The good thing about it is, again, you're opening the aperture, and you're actually identifying more people with the skills. So you might have a better, or at least a larger pool, but you still have to do more work to find the good candidates, and if you're looking for the exact right fit, there naturally will be more misaligned candidates than ideal candidates. As the volume increases, so does the amount of time and energy required to sift and sort. Even the best decision-makers experience fatigue. No one has infinite energy; you may read 999 resumes when the very best candidate was the 1,000th. This brings up a liability issue too, because you can't exclude people because you didn't get around to reading their resume.

Isn't sifting and sorting a place where our technology can help? What about AI? Depending on its quality, AI can help on some levels, if it's well-constructed and suited to your organization's needs, and your particular open position.

AI is a wonder. It can have conversations. It can translate language. It can extract meaning between words and ideas. It can retrieve and rank so that you can define a handful of criteria that are important in a candidate: I'm looking for people who went to Baylor; I'm looking for people who have a green card; I'm looking for people who have a certification in Microsoft Office. It can read through resumes and rank the candidates in the order of preference or in the order of match to those predefined criteria. It can also follow the tone of your conversation or can convert your speech to text. There are a multitude of things that AI does today and much it will do in the future: visual recognition, risk stratification, emotion analysis, and more. What it cannot adequately do is alert you to misinformation or skewed data; it works with the information and biases it's given.

What blockchain does is different. It offers a new level of verification and cross-checking. It provides a level of trust through verification protocol. That is inherently a function of the way blockchain is constructed as a technology.

AI works with the information candidates report themselves; blockchain compiles and verifies information independently of the candidate. That fundamental aspect of trust and verification is what needs to be solved in a world brimming with talent, tapped and untapped.

Imagine a search for a CFO. You'll need some criteria for distinguishing the level of quality among applicants. Blockchain is one step ahead. It will automatically confirm that this person was in a specific job, has certain certificates, has no history of financial fraud, has good credit history, and all of those other details that may be critical.

If that is the information you want validated about that candidate, it can be validated automatically and instantly before you go into time-consuming follow-ups and interviews. Now, think beyond the basics. Say you narrow down your candidates to the point where you are using past performance as a measure of fitness for the position. You could compare the candidates' companies' performance, which is a different data set, right? That can also be validated.

Public companies have their accounts or ledgers available, so you can verify their performance. For private companies, that may not be available. So how do you really know? Blockchain can put together the different pieces of verifiable information. Ultimately, when all these are linked together, you would be able to know that the person you're interviewing has the verified credentials and can also look at a true picture of how her or his previous companies performed. In addition to solving the egregious examples we've all heard of (people posing as doctors who wind up performing surgery without even having graduated medical school or politicians fraudulently claiming to have graduated cum laude from Ivy League universities), the trust and verification provided, is the more complex, nuanced potential of blockchain as it grows and becomes more accessible.

It's a burgeoning solution to the challenges of a world of potential talent: an overwhelming number of candidates and, yet, a supply and demand problem. There is human capability and potential, but what is missing without blockchain is a way to give people access to those opportunities and connect them in a way to find people with the right skill sets or working to gain the right skill sets. This is a clearly identifiable, data-driven issue in marginalized communities.

ATUL KNEW he wanted to teach, someday. He wanted to change things, for everyone.

"The years of subsistence farming, dealing with the cycle of drought and limited resources, showed me that technology could change things dramatically. Science could help everyone—better seeds, better crops, less poverty, and less hunger. Engineering seemed like a great field to study, but how?"

Atul had no idea how to figure out everything he needed to apply and be accepted into an engineering college. There was no one to help him understand how to navigate the world of higher education, outside their village. He studied every night outside Baiji's house and sometimes woke to find that she had put a blanket over him, keeping the dew and mosquitos away. But it paid off because Atul became the first person in the village to finish school with a distinction. It didn't matter under what light Atul studied.

Overjoyed, the village organized a felicitation ceremony headlined by their Member of the Legislative Assembly (MLA). "Everyone was very happy, but I still wasn't sure what came next for me. Now what? Where do I go from here?"

During the felicitation ceremony, speeches were made, and the statue of Gandhiji was garlanded. Fortunately, the

MLA announced that Atul would receive a scholarship to attend engineering college.

"I was just lucky I got the opportunity to move forward. The scholarship helped me leave and go to college."

WHEN YOU THINK about the US economy and talent field, many of its best and brightest have historically come from outside the country—and those are typically immigrants who have access to apply to the right universities. There are probably thousands of equally smart or smarter people who just didn't have the lucky stakes in life to apply to the right college. I grew up in India at a time when it was not easy to apply to the United States to do testing and pay those hefty application fees. It takes privilege and work to do that. If we could scale up the access to match the available talent, we would progress much faster. If we were able to tap into everyone's potential, we could all be much more successful.

Again, that's where blockchain can offer solutions.

Think again of how people are finding jobs today. A lot of it is still through networks, which is another reason why you need something more equitable—not just more equitable but also something more productive and more useful than, say, your dad's Rolodex. Those already connected people may not be the best people for your job. How do you move past that? How do you connect to the people who don't have that access? When you move out to sprawling online networks like LinkedIn, you get, once again, bogged down in sheer numbers. We need a better way to create access but also to sort, qualify, and vet those overwhelming talent pools—oceans in today's market —to find the right people.

This Universal Talent Exchange will continue to provide more access for more people, especially as we look at the degree of untapped talent in developing countries and those who are not currently formally employed. That will continue to grow and present challenges of scale. Blockchain provides an answer to many of those challenges and also offers a vehicle to disrupt harmful socioeconomic cycles in ways that happen to also benefit growing companies. Everything we, as recruiters, or those involved in the talent sphere need to make decisions can go on the blockchain.

Once a person's credentials are on the blockchain, and as blockchain grows beyond consortiums to a larger chain of information, those of us on the hiring side can quickly access verified and validated information that spans everything we may need to know. The entire cycle of everything that an individual does in employment—finding a job, being screened for it, publishing a paper or a book, working on a gig-based project, completing a course or certification—all of that would be enabled and accessible instantly and seamlessly by the blockchain. Of course, it comes with some inherent risks, some similar to what we face and now accept, with using the internet: identity, security, and safety, to name a few. Also similar to the internet, blockchain is moving inevitably toward one day becoming a necessity. Those who understand how best to maximize its potential for good, and learn how to implement protection and precaution, will be at an advantage. So, for now, let's focus on what it can open up for us.

As Atul argued with the proctor outside the exam hall, he felt so unlike himself. He had never raised his voice. He had always tried to be compliant. But this time, he had to speak—for his Aai, Baiji, Veer, the MLA, everyone who had helped him get here. Even Kiran the taxi driver. Kiran had dropped Veer and him at the correct bus stop, then waited until the double decker lumbered by. He saw them hop on the bus, and waved them off. Now, Atul was finally here, and he knew he had to write the exam.

As the registrar, Mr. Ganpat walked by, he overheard the argument. "Oh, let him in. Don't give him any extra time, but let him write," the registrar directed the proctor.

Atul felt overwhelmed with gratitude, and he dashed into the exam hall. I looked up from my paper and saw Atul dart into the seat next to me. I shook my head in sympathy, we smiled at each other, and I went back to writing.

Blockchain Can Alleviate Three Key Pain Points

Blockchain provides a way to authenticate who we are, what we do, our credentials, and our history or background. In a global field of talent, blockchain offers an elegant solution as the seamless digital passport or digital resume of the near future.

Provenance: In terms of data control, third parties validate candidate data. But people want control over their data, so they can share it when they want, without having to deal with a slow request process (think about the amount of time transcript requests from systems of higher education often require). Plus, they (candidates, job seekers) want to be in control of where the data goes and ensure that it won't be misused. Similarly, employment and background checks take time and require multiple transactions, especially to verify credentials and degrees from around the world.

Immutability: Employers need to request transcripts from universities, which takes time and sometimes costs a fee. There isn't a solid system for validating data about an individual's credentials, which increases the risk of fraud. Blockchain technology can actually confirm, validate, and authenticate an individual's achievements into a quantifiable skill score. Similarly, it can validate experiences, skills, and capabilities. These immutable records allow greater confidence and agility in making decisions.

Decentralization: On average, there are twenty-seven digital identities per person. With no single version of the truth, it's an ongoing challenge for employers and candidates to maintain accurate and up-to-date identity records. Using the public and private key, all participants in the network can provide validation without relying on a third party.

So, How Would a Universal Talent Exchange Work?

The easiest way to visualize the Universal Talent Exchange is to use an imperfect metaphor—that of LinkedIn on blockchain. The Universal Talent Exchange is different (and better) in that everything you access and store is valid and accurate, you are "self-sovereign" and own the data (not LinkedIn), and you control what is shared with whom.

Now, let's pivot to our Universal Talent Exchange or UTEX. It starts with federated, disparate consortiums of trusted nodes (participants) that agree to exchange information and validate it using a blockchain network and mutually agreed-upon rules. The consortium agrees on who will be the network operator and how the nodes participate in validation. Individuals or organizations use an application programming interface (API) to access the blockchain.

Remember, an API comprises the "rules and tools" to access data, interact, and build software.

A concierge or travel agent takes your Disneyland vacation idea and creates a plan that works for your family. You don't have to understand the pricing mechanism of every Disney meal plan or strategies to get on rides; instead, they bring what works for you. Similarly, APIs allow you to access technology without writing code each time. APIs help you use your voice to access the functions of Alexa—you don't have to write code or create software for voice recognition in order to play "Baby Shark" on repeat.

The consortium that sets up the network also enables digital passports for users with a software application. These digital passports have (among other components for health, banking, etc.) a validated record of all the skills and experiences acquired—the talent passport—think of it like a page/component of your digital passport. A talent passport is the validated record of all projects, assignments, tasks, slides, code, intellectual property, and articles authored.

Individuals access the UTEX through a portal, which provides access to the ecosystem. The portal will allow the sharing of their credentials, protected appropriately per data and privacy standards.

Educators and issuers provide information about learning options, media, and access channels. Individuals can take assessments for aptitude and skills levels, research career frameworks, and educate themselves on how to navigate from one skill level to another. They can also access information on the relationships between skill levels, courses, and careers. Individuals choose courses, gain credentials, and store them in their talent passport.

Educators, schools, colleges, and learning providers can enroll students and **issue** bonafides or credentials to learners on the blockchain. Think of these as stamps on your passport. Colleges can recruit people into their programs based on existing skills. Professional licensing organizations, Series 7, licensing boards for physicians, pilots, and veterinarians can all issue credentials and sign up to be part of a consortium as verifiers. Educators act as issuers, obviously, but also as validators for consensus.

Employers can **search and access** these validated credentials to hire people more easily. They can post skill requirements for gigs or jobs. Employers also issue credentials based on employment tenure, role, and so on, which are added to that talent passport.

Consistency on skill definitions and standards will make it easier to understand what we mean, across countries and languages. A common understanding and standards on the pathways for careers will allow people to understand how to navigate to greater levels of skill enhancement and opportunity. Individuals can participate in the consortium to share and validate their data; you can choose to participate in a consortium that will capture and validate all your educational credentials and work with your potential employer to provide it accurately, when you choose.

There may be multiple consortiums that start to do all of this, within their trusted networks. They may have their own payment methods using tokens or a similar mechanism. Consortium participants enroll to get the benefits of exchanging data. Others may participate to do the "proof of work" of validation and others may seek to invest in it, as a business idea that can be monetized by hosting data and information.

As these many smaller networks shift to agreeing on trust protocols to link up, and more and more consortiums integrate, we will have a global blockchain network that hosts and exchanges information seamlessly. While these credentialing networks exchange information, they can interface with web-based applications to make the interface easy and intuitive for users. Applications to store their credentials, applications to search for credentials (at the desired level of security), applications to validate and pay, all become available. Think of these applications like the web pages we use to access the underlying technology that fuels the internet. This is no different. The magic of this connectivity is that we provide a validated, level playing field for all.

∾

TWENTY-FIVE YEARS LATER, on a Saturday morning, Dr. Atul Jagat and I caught up on Zoom as Atul was heading back home from work. It was late evening in Wardha, India. I caught glimpses of the streets in Wardha from the video call, which he took from the backseat of his car. I watched him get out of his car and tell his driver when to come back in the morning. He switched to his laptop once he sat down on his couch. Atul's son Ajit sat on the arm of the couch, listening as we caught up. Atul had come a long way. After getting his PhD and teaching for a while, Atul became a university registrar in Ghana and the UAE, and now had finally come closer to home, to Wardha. I was curious about his role.

"I see myself as an advocate. I am the bridge between the students, teachers, and administrators. When I was younger it was always impossible to access all those opportunities. There is so much talent out there, so many people struggle needlessly. It shouldn't be so hard."

BLOCKCHAIN ALLOWS us to broaden and improve the spectrum and quality of talent available for positions and skills that are increasingly in-demand and often pivotal to growth; on the other side, it opens up access to communities of people who otherwise would remain undiscovered or restricted by a rigid socioeconomic hierarchy.

FOUR

Blockchain and People Data

I HATED WAKING up to the smell of kerosene. The smell meant the mandated daily glass of milk would be steeped with the flavor of smoky kerosene, and no amount of Boost would mask the odor.

In post-independence India, the monsoons determined the fate of farmers and the food supply. Buffeted by the cycle of floods, drought, and famine, the government issued ration cards. These ration cards were proof of identity, address, tenancy rights and family connection as they documented the names and birthdates of all in the family. These multi-page booklets, covered in plastic, also provided access to the government-supplied essentials. If you were migrant labor from the villages, or refugees from the 1971 war, all of whom streamed into Bombay, you probably didn't have a ration card, simply because no one could verify who you really were.

Government-owned ration shops sold each card-holding family a small monthly amount of a few basic food items like rice, wheat, oil, sugar, and "Ghaslet"[1] or kerosene. The quality was not great, but they were at reduced rates. Kerosene, which most families used for cooking, was available only in the ration shops due to fuel shortages. Each month's purchase was recorded in the booklet, so no one got more than their due. You could, of course, buy better quality essentials from the grocery stores if you could afford them.

Chinnu gave away most of the ration-card supplies to the "bai(s)"—women who worked as household help in our neighborhood. The "bai"[2] was the backbone of the urban household, especially as more women like Chinnu entered the workforce. In most apartment buildings, water flowed through taps only at certain times of the day per the municipality's schedule. In some homes, the bai had to come in time to turn on taps and store water in large plastic tubs, then use it to wash the dishes and clothes by hand. If (like in most homes) there was no washing machine, the bai washed everything, beat the clothes with a long wooden paddle, soaked the whites in a solution of *neel*,[3] then wrung and hung them on lines to dry. They swept and mopped floors, dropped us to school, and made hot *phulkas*[4] for dinner. These women were usually migrant labor from the villages, without a ration card and supporting large families. They all knew to come to our apartment if they needed anything, anytime.

Chinnu gave away a lot, but kept a small amount of kerosene to tide us over between empty cooking gas cylinders. On some days I would wake up to the smell of kerosene, which signaled that the big red replacement gas cylinder had not arrived. This also meant angst in the kitchen at the supply chain breakdown, and more morning tumult as Chinnu and the maid juggled between the smoky stove and the electric hotplate.

The grownups were quick to remind me that most people did *all* their cooking on kerosene stoves (or wood) every day. And reminded me that I should be grateful that we had a ration card, our proof of address, unlike many others. Though as an eight-year-old dawdling over sips of kerosene-flavored milk, I did not appreciate the value of the ration card, I do now.

Back in the 1970s, ration cards were issued and used to make a judgment call about who had legitimate identity and could buy kerosene. Bartenders, hotel clerks, librarians, and others in gatekeeper roles still carry out this process on a regular basis —making decisions about official paperwork you may carry around in your wallet. This is certainly not foolproof, as we all know, with the legion of fake ID stories among teenagers. So, consider the way the potential for problems has increased when we move the process to an online format. Instead of a human in a face-to-face interaction with someone looking for access or approval, you have a machine. That machine is not inspecting a physical document but a digital one.

The challenge that is central to how we transact business and collaborate in a virtual environment (and over the internet) on a global scale is the lack of a consistent and accurate method to verify digital credentials. How do we know who we are transacting with? How do we verify who we are? And do we really know who the other party is?

How can we create the tools to verify a digital credential? We can't do that with any certainty if the format is not first standardized. If we are going to have machines as gatekeepers and inspectors, we need to be submitting information in ways a machine can understand. This already happens on some level. Take a look at your passport and you'll see that it includes sections that are machine-readable. Your ATM card does the same. But we also need a standardized way to provide verification. This, too, already happens with the government or your bank issuing credentials. Your bank also issues digital signatures. Those require two "keys" to be accepted in most jurisdictions: a private/signing key, which is kept secret by the issuer (your ATM code), and a public/verification key (your ATM card or app), which ensures that the document has not been altered and that the document itself is not secret. Again, it comes down to the need for standardization. To be able to rely on digital credentials to use in virtual spaces, we need to agree upon a universal format to verify the issuer's key and authenticate the credential.

One solution that has been offered is the public key infrastructure (PKI).[5] The validity of the PKI relies on the validity of two cryptographically linked keys—one private and one public. The core challenge is the validity and accuracy of each unique public key, a challenge that has been solved through PKI for the past twenty years.

Many of us have seen this before, perhaps without realizing it. The indicator is the small green padlock situated before the URL line in modern browsers. If you see this symbol, it means that a certificate authority has received a public key from a website, which owns both a private and public key, issued through a public key certificate. Your browser tells you that you are viewing or inter-acting on a website with an encrypted connection and has gone through this secure verification process.

The problem is that this is centralized. It's a process and service that can't be provided on a global scale because it's not standardized and decentralized. Those certificates are too time-consuming and costly to be replicated and, more importantly, verified on every site. Those certifi-cate authorities are the keepers of trust, built into browsers and privately owned software. Adding a middleman weakens the level of trust and compromises digital trust infrastructure. So the certificate authorities and private companies remain in control of this vital step toward being able to work, hire, and grow globally.

Let's break this all back down to the human level again. We're really talking about the simple exchange of information; protecting and verifying it on a larger scale than the ways we have operated for thousands of years.

Essentially, the wanderbuch was a beta version of what we might call a resume. Journeymen carried them around from place-to-place, and people stamped them to certify that they had done a job, had demonstrable, and proven skills, and the journeymen would be able to show that to the next potential client in the neighboring town.

That offered some early form of validity, or at least a list of credentials. Because they were traveling in small locations, not globally, it was manageable, and people trusted the information that the journeymen provided. That morphed into resumes, which, importantly, don't require any outside stamp of approval or other type of certainty. The reason we have resumes is because people come from all over. We're no longer hiring from the next neighborhood or village; we're working far beyond our personal networks (though those, of course, still come into play).

Then there is the validation of the resume, which still needs to happen through background checks or educational qualifications. We need to make sure it's real, valid, and true. Many of us are guilty of at least shining up how we present ourselves on paper to a potential employer, and some of us are guilty of slight embellishments. Almost all of us know of a case or two where applicants have outright lied.

Because we have evolved to a global field of talent, the need for swift, independent verification is more pressing than it's ever been before. It's time for the digital passport and, related but not exactly the same, the skills passport.

What do I mean by that? Think about the sheer amount of information that exists online about any one of us. We don't think about the bits of data floating out there with every social platform when we create a profile or even with every website with cookies that we visit. These are more than snippets of information; they make up who we are in a digital world.

Data defines your identity. This includes the indicative data about yourself and the data you collect as you work, too: your skills, education, employment, background checks, and so on. Blockchain will lead to the rise of an organized, verified collection of this information, the digital passports, the new digital wanderbuchs that describe your life in data sets. Think of all your versions of resumes, all your certificates, all your academic honors—all collected in a streamlined digital report card, a digital and chronological picture of your life. Digital passports are your life digitized, a reflection of your online identities, your digital footprint—all of which already exists, currently unpoliced and unguarded on the World Wide Web.

The digital passport is linked to our digital footprint, which we have not always had, but as we become more active on the internet and in the virtual digital world, we begin to leave a trail of cookies: which sites we visit, what identities we have online, what email addresses we use, who we've completed transactions with, and what handles we create and photos we post.

Your digital passport is almost like your real passport, which captures key pieces of information that you may need to travel physically. Your metadata—all those small actions and pieces of information collected about you—helps you operate and transact in the digital world and also creates a digital version of your person. Your journey across the cyber world is really your digital footprint. Everywhere we go (virtually), we leave a trail. Companies are happy to pick up what you leave behind.

Our personal data is a goldmine, and we donate it on a daily basis. The numbers are beyond what our minds can fathom: Companies scoop up some 2.5 quintillion bytes of data every single day from internet users. Who decides how it's used? Private companies—centralized platforms that share among themselves in any way they see fit. The result is that companies crunch this valuable data, use it to guide business decisions and make billions in profit, and influence those same internet users who gave up their information, mostly unwittingly, and at no cost.

How could we, instead, put the value of our digital lifestyles to work to benefit us? Why should private companies be the primary beneficiaries of the systems we have in place and we all use?

The Digital Passport (Leveling Up)

A digital passport is, or will be, a more comprehensive, structured, secure way to share and authenticate information in a way that accurately captures your skills, training, education, and work history. Of course there needs to be some level of security associated with it, some authentication, which is what blockchain can provide. That's what makes the digital passport more valuable or important...because it is authenticated. The two, blockchain and digital passports, are interconnected.

In many ways, what we're doing when we apply blockchain to any transaction is basically validating the accuracy of that transaction. Let's take something as simple as your high school degree or GED. Where is the record of that? Hopefully, at your high school. Maybe I have a paper certificate that says, this is Elizabeth, she has a high school diploma, and these were the credits she earned, and she graduated in this year from this school. That's how I could prove that I attended and completed high school.

But what if it's a fake copy? Those pieces of paper are not hard to replicate, so you need an official copy, which won't arrive at a hiring manager's office on the same day it's requested, by any means. Even after it shows up, if my counterfeit skills are fairly decent, you may not know for sure. You'd have to make a personal judgment call.

Therein lies the dilemma, right? I have to have some record that I can show you, and one that doesn't require you to personally go and authenticate with my high school principal, who may not remember I was even there.

Now, the way a digital password would operate in the blockchain environment is that the authentication would already exist in that passport. So, if you're trying to figure out if I have a high school degree, I will share a key by which you can access this digital passport I own. Then you can read that section of my history and know with certainty that I successfully completed high school. It's validated. It's available instantly. It's almost like a notarized document, and the trust around the data that I'm providing is authenticated. In the world of blockchain, our digital passports will have verified data, which will help us identify ourselves. That's why the security of this technology is so important.

Our educational history is really just the baseline. As anyone who has added a badge to their LinkedIn profile may realize, we have to prove our skills. Our abilities can't be captured in a degree or even simply with a list of our work history. We need to be able to demonstrate what we have done or can do. You may have learned a version of this when you were a kid, if you were a member of the Boy Scouts or Girl Scouts of America. Earn your badge—display it proudly.

Beyond digital passports, skills passports go deeper into describing who you are: they are the LEGO blocks of the skills you have garnered, your visible badges that describe the various skills you have acquired. The scouts were probably the first to parse skills like tracking in the wild. Somebody took the time to aggregate and formalize life skills, such as surviving in the wilderness, and thought about the real-world requirements: What do you need to survive in the wilderness? How do you start a fire? How do you read a compass?

And then they actually provided a whole path to acquiring those buildable life skills through a series of badges. A lot of the work we're seeing today in badging and learning emerges from that idea, which worked really well. It connected learning with a visible reward, a point of pride. The principles of online gaming also rely heavily on these psychological rewards, whether it's Minecraft or some other virtual world.

Each level and badge builds on the last, and other participants can see what you've achieved. That became a great way to engage gamers and show them progression. Similarly, the learning industry took the baton and started providing certifications: You can now capture your ongoing learning, in addition to what is indicated by formal education degrees. It's a distinguishing factor, even though it, too, can be flawed. We all know that having an MBA doesn't automatically make you a brilliant business person. In the same way, having taken a class on ethics does not indicate that you are an honest person. There's potential fallacy in the current badging opportunities, but at least it records that you have completed certain agreed-upon requirements. We already use badges to map learning levels and skills. As with digital passports, blockchain again provides a means to independently verify these badges.

And skills are becoming more and more important.

Across the board, jobs are becoming more complex with the infusion of technology. If you're a marketing person, it isn't enough to just understand consumer behavior. You have to understand technology, analytics, digital marketing, and search engine optimization. You also often navigate certain sets of software. The work that a marketing person does has become multidisciplinary. The same is true for people on the shop floor. Factory workers in many places are actually operating robots; they're not doing the work by hand, so the skill is no longer directly definable by the job. As work becomes more complex, and particularly with the rapid pace of technological change, the way work has to be done has transformed again and again. You cannot really rely on a base degree to keep you updated on your chosen field of work.

What becomes really important in this context is ongoing skill acquisition. Think about the recent past: In the 1990s, as people started getting certified on Microsoft, people realized you need to know certain technologies and ways to code and manage data. Skill acquisition on an ongoing basis has, I would say, become more important than your basic degree because the rubric is changing all the time, and that pace is only going to accelerate.

To keep up, you need to map the right skill acquisition, and how do you do that on an ongoing basis? Badges are a means to demonstrate recent and ongoing career development.

This kind of evolution is something we can't avoid if we're going to survive, no matter how great your product or service. If you're a company selling the best hand-knit baby blankets, you're limited in your sales figures if you don't figure out how to sell them on Etsy or another online avenue so that people outside your town can buy them. The same thing is true for bigger and more complex organizations; they have to quickly pivot and teach people new things or hire people who know how to perform those new tasks.

In that situation, what is really important, then, is authenticating the skill acquisition. This has happened already organically. Think of Degreed, which has learning badges that you can display on your LinkedIn profile. You might show that you are Microsoft certified, have learned the latest version of PowerPoint, or even that you've taken a wine tasting course. Or you might learn through Coursera. Or Udemy. The process has already started.

In all those situations, authentication is really important. The means to instantly validate your credentials is where blockchain comes in again.

This brings us back to the three principles or pain points that blockchain solves. The first is the principle of *provenance*, which is really knowing where something comes from. It's the same concept of looking up the provenance of a piece of art. Was it stolen? Did it originate from a reliable source? What journey did it take to get from artist to the institution where you are right now?

So then the provenance of that degree, knowing that it is verified from and by the educational institution it was supposed to originate from, is actually very important.

The second is the principle of *immutability*, which means the information history cannot be changed. Once you have a degree or certification recorded on blockchain, you can add to the record to indicate modification, but you cannot alter the reality that it was there. Somebody may go in and say that degree was fake or, alternatively, the degree was true, but there will be a record of the query, challenge, or additional information. Everything is linked, like LEGO blocks, and the trail of information and even allegations and challenges are there.

You can also record if there is any kind of decision or contract. Blockchain creates that path, that chain of LEGO blocks, and shows that there was a decision point. As progress around an agreement is made, you can clearly and easily see the path forward.

The third principle is the benefit of *decentralization* —or a broad range of sources. With the decentralized nature of blockchain, it's not one person or one organization who is the arbitrator of a person's identity.

Blockchain moves us from individual and small-scale sharing to a verified, decentralized ledger. Remember that the ledger is not a complex or new concept: a record of exchanges of goods and services between two individuals. That can expand into a distributed ledger, a recorded history of exchanges among multiple parties, viewable by anyone in a network. The blockchain further combines the elegant simplicity of those two concepts, creating a digital distributed ledger that is tailored to the needs of a broader community and standardized so it is efficient and usable to all parties involved.

The Sovrin Foundation

They used to say that each person has twenty-seven versions of their digital identity, but that number is outdated and probably far below our true reality. Imagine all those different versions converging into one verified version, without a single source dictating final decisions. They all come into play.

The decentralization aspect of blockchain circumvents the need for one central approval and also allows for multiple organization types to add to my digital passport—not just a single school or higher ed institution. All of those transactions, from education to skills to work history, are linked and verified in a way that we might compare to notarization.

Now, undertaking an organized approach to this, with ambitions of making it accessible on a globally connected level is no small task. It's far more advantageous, though, than allowing blockchains to spontaneously happen. The Sovrin Foundation,[6] an international nonprofit undertook this effort, publishing a relevant white paper in 2018.

The economic and social implications are so far reaching; it's a space that we must get in front of. According to the World Bank, about one seventh of the world's population has no legal identity. Think about the lack of access and opportunity for those people—or of the human rights crises that arise from those populations that are unseen: kidnapping, forced labor, trafficking, and other travesties. How do we provide a system that accounts for and protects those people, that meets everyone's needs, and that does not leave all the cards with companies or consortiums with all means of control and access? This is bigger than a single company or even a single nation. We must work beyond boundaries to create a system that provides opportunity and security on a global scale. We need a global public utility, designed in a way that does not make cost a barrier to access. The Sovrin Foundation affirms that the goal must be to provide identity for all.

That also means it must meet the strictest and highest privacy standards in the world, provided by the EU's General Data Protection Regulation, the toughest privacy and security law in existence. Privacy must be the foundation or such a system could create widespread harm rather than protection and access for the individual.

The work IBM has done with the Digital Health Pass,[7] which enables companies to verify health credentials for employees and visitors, offers a model for protecting the privacy of sensitive information in the workplace and elsewhere, while still performing an important function. It allows organizations to simply download an app to begin the process. An issuer can add credentials for an individual: medical test results, temperature checks, vaccination records, and the like. A verifier checks off an individual's requirements, submitted by the issuer, and allows access to a certain facility if the requirements are met. This can be used to confirm COVID-19 test results or vaccinations, but the implications are much broader. The parties involved are limited to individuals, verifiers, and issuers, and IBM does not store any personally identifiable information on the Digital Health Pass blockchain platform.

Issuers package the data they want to include, and a programming interface cryptographically signs the credential with the issuer's secret key and then wraps it as a verifiable credential. A credential, therefore, is a document that has been signed and anchored by the issuer's decentralized identifier in the blockchain ledger. Personal information stays securely encrypted in the app on an individual's phone. Individual credential holders remain in complete control of what information is shared and with whom.

When it comes to privacy measures, there is a lot of work to be done—and if we don't all step up to do it, someone else will. This is our chance to have a say in shaping how the blockchain comes together. It's critical to secure self-sovereign identity to address the issues that arise with the proliferation of digital footprints. The scope for fraud and insecurities is enormous and a protocol must be established, for the safety of us all.

These considerations on identity and security will also be accelerated by the three developments I mentioned in Chapter 1. First, the rise of *quantum computing* with its impact on data processing and encryption.[8] Second, the speed of *space exploration* with its implications on industry, geopolitics, security and very remote work.[9] Third, the origami horizons of the *Metaverse*.[10] Each of these developments accelerate and alter our ability to connect.

All magnify the need for real trust. I'll touch on these *very* briefly here, as each needs a separate and deep conversation we can pick up another time.

1. *Quantum for Solace, Or Not*

In a year marked by the unveiling of "The Osborne 1," the first successful portable computer and, airing of the first MTV music video, the lock-picking, samba-loving percussionist Richard Feynman proposed a new machine. He proposed a "universal quantum simulator" that would use quantum principles to run simulations[11] to overcome the limitations of classical computing.

Now the roots of this idea and machine go back to 1871 when James Clerk Maxwell imagined a sentient being or device (later called Maxwell's Demon) that was capable of detecting and reacting to the motions of individual molecules.[12]

Over the next sixty years, we saw clarification of the elegant and confounding principles[13] of "Superposition" and "Entanglement" that anchor quantum mechanics. Now, Superposition is the ability of quantum bodies to be in two different states at the same time. For an electron, this means that it has the probability to be a little excited and a lot excited at the same time, with this duality ceasing the instant we measure its energy level!

The equally intriguing "quantum entanglement" is the inexplicable connection such that the quantum state of one, cannot be completely independent of the other's. Einstein called this entanglement as "spooky action at a distance" because the particles appear to communicate faster than light across distances.[14] Perhaps the premise of every Hallmark movie as well?

The shift from the "bits" of classical computing to "qubits" helped us construct quantum computers that exponentially increase the speed and accuracy with which we can steer meaning into multiple and very large data sets. We do this by enhancing some probabilities (the correct ones) and suppressing others (wrong answers) to maximize the probability of correct answers.

There's a lot of work being done to apply quantum solutions to complex challenges. Scientists are building a quantum laser system that will relay information to the International Space Station, using entangled photons of light that would transfer information over large distances without loss.[15] Scientists at Fermi and Argonne labs are also working "entanglement swapping" on their journey to build what they hope will be the quantum internet, while quantum interferometry is being used to study our planet.[16] The use of quantum computing is moving into the mainstream and will transform our understanding and use of molecular biology, material sciences, energy, traffic patterns, financial models, and any complex data set.

In addition, quantum computing will result in acceleration in AI and machine learning, anchored by neural networks. This will require more governance and validation of human versus machine identity.

This same power of quantum computing and its increasing use also has the potential to diminish the utility of encryption methods used today,[17] like PKI, which we talked about earlier in this chapter. A classical computer with one trillion operations per second, would need about three hundred trillion years to break the commonly used RSA2048-bit encryption. This could be done by a quantum computer using Shor's algorithm in ten seconds. Yes, ten seconds. Other methods of cryptographic hashing are not as susceptible, but shortcuts like Grover's algorithm, which use "brute-force search," can diminish their security as well. Consequently, we will rapidly see the need for post-quantum encryption to validate and protect self-sovereign identity.

2. No Barriers in the Final Frontier (of Space Exploration)[18]

The skies above us are getting crowded. Constellations of satellites twinkle and traverse the Low Earth Orbit (LEO), dodging clumps of space debris and stray asteroids. More and more vehicles plunge into the upper reaches of our atmosphere as well, in a "Space Scramble" that grows more intense daily, reflected in the tremendous growth in investments and commerce. This economy that operates in space was 447 billion USD[19] in 2020, expected to be as much as 3 trillion USD by 2040.[20]

So what exactly is going on?

Space has been democratized as every nation and many companies reach upward to access the skies above us. There is recognition of the potential in harnessing Earth observation data, which when manipulated by AI and quantum computing will give us new insights into challenges as varied as flood management to malarial mitigation to defense. More and more private companies are working to leverage the benefits of operating in space. More than 7,500 satellites are in LEO today,[21] providing Earth imagery and supporting television, geolocation, and navigation. We see the emergence of space mining, space tourism, traffic jams, and near collisions in the skies above us. Recall the recent complaints from the Chinese space station Tiangong about a near miss with a Space X satellite.

The decades-long work of the SETI Institute was accelerated with NASA's 2021 Mars rover Perseverance that searches for microbial evidence on the red planet. Meanwhile, a privately funded research initiative led by MIT will launch a mission in 2023 to expand on the research to explore the potential presence of Phosphine and other chemical anomalies on Venus.[22] The United States[23] and China will build lunar habitats over the next few years. NASA's Moon to Mars program geared toward sustainable human presence on the moon is to prepare for future human missions to Mars.

All this extra-planetary activity and presence will only accelerate, as more commercial players and more nation states participate. The price and barriers to participation will continue to drop. An example of this is the Indian Mars mission Mangalayan, which at 67 million USD, cost less than the what it took to make the Hollywood movie *Gravity*! Its cost was also a fraction of the cost of NASA's Mars Maven, which cost 583 million USD.[24]

This global progress and participation will also have corollary implications on security and defense, which will further the interest and pace of space exploration. Ultimately this will compound the need for solutions to validate and trust as we work and collaborate virtually across inter-planetary distances.

3. The Obverse of an Adverse Metaverse

In his 1992 novel, *Snow Crash*, Neal Stephenson first described the Metaverse as the "same sort of wireless, online virtual-reality experience that Facebook, Google, Samsung, and practically every other major tech company are now competing to commercialize." In an interview, Stephenson told Vanity Fair that he was just "making s*&% up."[25] But, today the Metaverse is more plausible.

The Metaverse describes the combination of augmented, virtual, and mixed reality fusing into "extended reality" (or XR), which changes our experience and perception of how we interact, when using technology.

Anyone who has played a video game (with real interest) knows that you experience a different reality as you fall through different lives and try to get your score up. Meanwhile, your brain retains and manages two realities: (1) your physical reality, where you sit, hold the gaming stick, lean back into your chair, and take a deep despairing breath; and (2) the reality of the video game where you think you are someplace else. The Metaverse will synchronize these realities by how technology is accessed and then integrated into your perceptions of experience and value.[26] Again, this integration of experience and realities already happens to a certain extent with video games and social platforms (some may even argue, in casinos or sports stadiums) where you enter different worlds, commit to and value different experiences, and participate in economic activity with other players.

The Metaverse then is the next evolution of the internet where we use XR to enhance the experience of a video call, a workout, a collaboration session, a movie, a political dialogue, or a concert. We will continue to use it for connection, transactions, to buy and sell (hamsters, vinyl records of Joni Mitchell, and NFTs), and all economic activity, and use it even more than we do today. The use of blockchain enhances utility by how it can manage payments and maintains integrity of individual discernment as well.

So what will remain the most important thing as we navigate what lies ahead?

Our identity. The ability to remain self-sovereign and control our information becomes even more critical. Blockchain can help us do that.

Fueled and driven by technology, we will entangle, and change how we live, work. A thoughtful, collaborative approach using blockchain solves one of the oldest and most challenging problems of the internet: our digital identity.

This affects all of us—and all digital versions of us.

FIVE

Blockchain in Recruitment

TAPPING into talent is among the most difficult challenges recruiters face. So is the verification process.

There are very obvious ways that verifying credentials come into play in the recruitment process—all those scenarios where someone might be going far beyond shedding the most positive possible light on their skills, education, or work history. I'm talking about bald-faced lies. In one frequently cited survey by CareerBuilder, 58 percent of hiring managers reported that they have caught an outright lie on a resume. Over a third of those respondents in that same survey said they had seen a notable increase in skill embellishment.

You can understand why this would be troublesome for hiring managers sitting down to interviews and then, past the interview, when the standard background check for a promising candidate might be a couple of calls to references, at most. Those references, of course, are provided by (and presumably influenced by) the candidate directly.

It also poses problems beyond recruitment and the hiring stage. I'll share one quick story from my own career.

This was about twenty years ago. We had hired someone a few years prior, and he recently transferred to my direct team. We had a really great tuition reimbursement program, and he decided to take advantage of it. All good, so far.

He traveled overseas and while there, took a course. It was a serious investment at the time by the company, something like $5,000. All he had to do was submit his receipt and the documentation afterward.

A couple months later came an awkward conversation. I had to confront him because our HR person had called me, concerned about the submitted paperwork. He told me he had taken the course. I had to push a little more. What documentation had he provided that prompted concern from our HR folks?

Apparently, rather than actually completing a course, this person created a fake certificate of payment for that course. Sharp eyes by our HR people helped crack the case. They were suspicious about the provenance of both the course and the certificate he presented. Not long after, he left the company, presumably without losing his fraudulently gained $5,000. That's the type of case where documents can fail us, despite our best, albeit human, efforts.

As (fallible) humans, we make judgment calls all the time. We trust our gut to tell us whether paperwork and documentation are legitimate or not, based on what we know the documentation should look like. The margin for error here is pretty wide, but this kind of system can work on a very small scale, within a company department or the like.

When we broaden that out to the scope of the entire globe, the margin for error explodes. We trust organizations, such as educational institutions, to respond to our requests for verification. When the verification arrives, we expect and care fairly certain of its provenance. But those steps require time and expense. That's why many institutions such as schools and employers do not verify much or all of an applicant's credentials.

This leaves us vulnerable, and that vulnerability gets taken advantage of. In a 2020 Ethical Hiring Alignment survey by Checkster, 78 percent of candidates admitted to lying on their resumes.[1] A 2021 survey by HireRight showed that 53 percent of employers in the United States reported that they had caught discrepancies on resumes through screening.[2] Globalization exacerbates the need for extensive verification: The market for employment background checks was about $5 billion in 2020, and is expected to double by 2028.[3] In addition to that, 73 percent of employers perform employment pre-hire checks, and 51 percent verify education certifications and credentials.

With blockchain, institutions would already have a distributed copy of the applicant's credentials and could trust its authenticity. All changes to resume, certifications, or training would be recorded on the chain for all permissioned participants to see. Schools, previous employers, and government agencies would have a copy of the applicant's resume and personal information, thus verifying its authenticity. Human resources would have a copy of the applicant's data, including the resume, as well as a historical copy of any changes—going as far back as the history of the chain. Any changes that the candidate would make to a resume or personal information would be verified by institutions before it would be shared with everyone with a copy of the ledger. Interviewers, therefore, could accurately rely on the content on the resume.

Instant. Trustworthy. Verified.

That's a game changer for organizations that need to move quickly and find the right people with the right skills. A fully developed blockchain, with across-the-board protocol implemented provides a solution to verifying credentials and the other top challenges facing recruiters right now in a global talent marketplace.

Think again of the environment that industry leaders and fledgling companies face today and how it affects talent management and recruitment.

Jobs have become very complex, so much so that there is a significant lack of clarity about what titles mean. The gig economy, consultants, and freelancers amassing projects and skills can exacerbate this issue. There are so many nuances to what most of us do for a living. The first problem is disaggregating a role into something that makes sense and is consistent, even within the organization. Often it's very hard to explain what jobs entail, and it's very hard for both job seeker and hiring manager to fully encapsulate job descriptions.

If my manager, for example, says, "Okay, this is what I need the person to do, and they need these skills," there is still a question of how different people even define a specific skill. Does that include tools you know how to use to perform that skill? Does it encompass a number of leadership skills? Can you perform the skill with technology or on your own? What's the common language around the job skills and positions you need?

That creates an immediate problem for the recruiter because they are trying to get clarity around the role they are seeking to fill. It's another reason we need to collaborate with others in the industry to create protocols, definitions, and parameters, so that we can measure, verify, and hire people with the skills our organizations actually need.

What recruiters are not suffering from is an insufficiency of candidates applying. Instead, they're actually suffering from a deluge of data, as we've discussed. They have so many resumes landing in their inbox, they cannot actually sift through and understand which are the best ones because there is information overload. In many cases, it's not humanly possible to really map all of those or even skim through that number of resumes, much less determine which ones are the best. They have to have an objective way of assessing and stack ranking the candidates in the order of their expertise or value. Basically, the problem is this: How do you manage the information coming at you and process it and make sense of it—especially when individuals and organizations aren't even defining things the same way?

The truth is that many hiring practices automatically screen out talent with less access. The access issue impacts the pipeline all the way back in terms of who actually enters the talent pipeline, which is entirely a function of economic ability, social privilege, historical precedent, and geography. This was quite evident in Atul's story, from our discussion on the talent exchange. The best candidate for a particular job might not have every attribute but might have the best attributes in the most critical area. The disaggregation of jobs into skills helps us focus on the most important attributes. Ultimately, this can help us decouple the requirements for formal or college degrees. This re-credentialing of jobs can help us open up a whole new pool of talent around the world.

This needs to be combined with skill-focused hiring processes and practices in organizations, along with skill-aligned career mobility, plus cultural acceptance and inclusion. Once we solve that, we can open the door to a whole new world in terms of opportunities for hiring and opportunities to increase access to more people.

Systems for comparison fall far short and often lead to scenarios where hiring managers are overlooking better candidates simply due to the overload of information, the complexity of jobs, and the lack of standardization of skills. It could even be due to candidates whose skill set do not fully or accurately present their abilities "on paper." We all know those types of hires, the good kind of surprise. They're better than you expect only because they aren't great at selling themselves. Those are exactly the types of candidates who would benefit from a verified, standardized track record.

As the hiring manager in the current situation, without blockchain, you are likely missing better candidates for a job. They are out there somewhere, and you may not be accessing them because you are mired in the overwhelming number of applicants or don't have access to an accurate picture of what they can do.

Say you're looking for high-value skills in cybersecurity. Suppose you identify cybersecurity professionals primarily among males because those are the people currently connected to you and sharing your job posting. In that case you're basically leaving half the candidate population by the wayside. You're limiting your funnel, and the quality of recruiting is going to decrease. That's another reason recruiters must figure out ways in which to eliminate bias, in even the most subliminal manner. Where did the job applicants come from? Where did they find you?

There has been a lot of research around recruiters ignoring names that sound African American or being more likely to perceive male names as candidates who are more competent.[4] Both of those are qualifiers human eyes pick up just by looking at the resume. Information pulled from validated skills from the blockchain eliminates many types of bias and ensures that you're opening the aperture for candidates of all kinds to enter through the funnel. Blockchain helps us solve the issues of accessing talent globally. It helps us access validated talent, no matter where in the world it happens to originate.

While blockchain can't directly help you with defining your job description, the consensus required to create a successful global blockchain may help us consider standardized approaches.

To achieve self-sovereign identity, we need to create a world that does not rely on brokers. Students should be able to provide access to verified achievements without being beholden to vendors or stuck with lengthy waiting periods. The other problem with these yet-to-be-developed products is that we don't know how they will employ open standards or public blockchains. This means it's probable that they will place us back into the issues of depending on privately developed, proprietary products that don't work across the board, are pay-to-play, and don't adapt well. Students have earned their credentials, and those verified records should be available to them and to potential employers for their entire career, not simply for the lifetime of a short-lived product.

There is a quote by Vitalik Burterin, co-founder of Ethereum and co-founder of *Bitcoin Magazine*, on the ability of blockchain to eliminate middlemen: "Instead of putting the taxi driver out of a job, blockchain puts Uber out of a job and lets the taxi driver work with the customer directly."

A number of notable private players have tried to make a bid for this kind of technology through partnerships or products on the way: Sony Global Education, Salesforce.org, Credly, Accredible, and others. Japanese subsidiary Recruit Technologies is another company that has announced plans to help increase transparency and curb fraud in some of these HR processes. The company's aim, at the time of the announcement, was to use a scalable blockchain database to position the offering for future growth.

Just because a company uses the term blockchain, or even if they use a blockchain framework, this is much different from what we might call *the* blockchain—an interconnected web of blockchains that are standardized and accessible without hefty fees, subscriptions, or purchases. Eventually, we need a blockchain that is decentralized, secure, and all-encompassing. To achieve self-sovereignty, we need both recipient ownership and vendor independence. Tying us indefinitely to networks controlled exclusively by a single private enterprise—or even to a university system itself, as some have proposed—will create indefinite problems.

Blockchain can help us transform many steps across the lifecycle of recruitment and, importantly, it also places a level of control back in the applicant's court. Do you know who has copies of your resume? How many versions of your resume have you sent out over the years? How many places did you upload these documents? How many pieces of paper with your name and grades float out there in someone's shredder, landfill, inbox? When you apply for a job, you send out your hopes and aspirations with your resume, not knowing where the data lands. Putting validated credentials and ensuring that they can be shared on an as-needed basis allows candidates to control who has access to their data.

Instead of paying for extra services like job boards, companies could work directly with candidates using a blockchain-based platform that hosts validated resumes. Incentives could be established to incentivize candidates to share their resumes directly.

As these technologies come to fruition, General Data Protection Regulation (GDPR) standards are also becoming more relevant. GDPR was implemented in the European Union to provide consistent standards for controlling an individual's own data. Currently, GDPR and its requirements only apply in the European Union, but many of the principles will become more required globally, which we will cover in greater depth later.

Blockchain is also an ideal solution for providing accurate background checks past the resume and interview stage. Candidates will be able to share information about their degrees easily and securely. When I was interviewing for a job, I had to affirm my degrees through an arduous process. First, the employer verified my name with the college, but then they needed to send the college the undergraduate and graduate college certificates I provided. This required me to dig those out from under paperwork and find a thirty-year-old document. Thankfully, it hadn't been lost. I sent in photos of those documents, which they sent to my colleges back in India. From there, we got back a request for a scanned copy, which I then sent. If the blockchain could host this validated data about my degree, I wouldn't have had to do any of that. Based on who needed to see it, I could provide the key for validation to view. Easy as that.

Today, in the United States, a lot of this happens through the National Student Clearinghouse and contact with individual schools and employers. The National Student Clearinghouse, Western

Governors University, Central New Mexico Community College, and IQ4, and IBM have come together to create an employment or credential verification, using blockchain[5] called the Learning Credential Network.[6]

Many players are also working to provide background check support. Typically, data is reviewed from multiple databases, such as criminal databases, Social Security number locators, sex offender records search, credit reports, among others. Blockchain can disrupt this entire complex system and allow candidates to manage their own profiles and provide access, as needed.

Again, we're not the only ones to realize the power of solving these pain points. Workday has launched a credentialing service built on a blockchain model. Their product, Credentials, is designed to ease the pains of this process. Background screening provider InfoMart has a product called Career Wallet so job candidates can save and oversee their credentials digitally, and MIT has launched a digital diploma pilot program, complete with an encrypted course certificate. Yet another private player, CVerification, offers decentralized background verification platforms.

Applicant screening platform, Veremark, also offers a solution to the problem of redundancy and inefficiency in the background screening market and the need for employers to keep rechecking that which has already been checked.

Through a user-friendly interface and integration with applicant tracking systems, Veremark has pioneered a platform that uses blockchain to increase the reliability and speed of getting checks done and returns the checked data back to the individual.

As part of its offering, the platform has brought to market the Veremark Career passport, which creates a means for an individual to own and share verified data with whomever they like. This can save the candidate time not only in the employment context but also in applying for a mortgage or rental property, applying for various courses or visas, and a wide range of other use cases.

This allows the hiring company the chance to show their forward-thinking attitude and give the verified data back to the now-checked employee as a benefit for having gone through the process, which adds to their employer brand proposition.

The same way that we could put degrees and credentials on the blockchain, we could also use it to hold test results, validated skills, licenses, and more. For example, suppose we put doctors' board certifications, state licenses, and credentials on a secure blockchain. In that case, data could be selectively accessed and viewed by a hospital system trying to make a hiring decision or even by a patient. We'll explore the linkage to learning credentials in more detail in the next chapter.

Why have so many companies stepped forward? The same reason the employment background check industry is poised to continue significant growth. There is an ongoing, multiplying need for credential verification in our hiring processes, for all the reasons we've discussed: globalization, exponential growth, and disruption within existing and emerging industries, changing trends in length of employment, the gig economy, and other factors that continue to reshape how we approach hiring. To reduce fraud and inefficiencies, a speedy, trustworthy process built on a decentralized public blockchain will help recruitment teams keep up and help their companies live up to their potential.

Most importantly, it can help us navigate a complex and increasingly, overwhelmingly broad field of talent by helping us with a longstanding, central dilemma of talent management: finding the best fit and knowing the people we're considering for the next hire are really who they say they are, with verifiable skill sets, education, and certifications. When you think about background checks or all the information that should be considered in the hiring decision, blockchain automatically provides that through keys and hashes shared securely across the network.

SIX

Blockchain in Learning

HAND-IN-HAND with the complexity of jobs and
confusion over job titles is the increasing relevance
of skills—and the increasing value of skills over
job titles and degrees. The underlying issue is that
new technologies and even new industries are
emerging as our world becomes broader. Our individual capabilities become even more important
than degrees, which are likely outdated, or even
job descriptions, which can fail to provide a true
picture of what a person did or does.

Degrees were created to indicate skills in a fundamental sense. The formality of their structure, the
"brand" names, and big names that come with
them have, in the past, provided some certainty of
accomplishment and ability. They remain a few
steps removed from the practicality of how the
skills they intend to demonstrate are gained by the
individuals who earned the degree.

I think we've all heard the trope that an MBA teaches you a lot but nothing useful. Or people go to college to do other things—make connections, prove themselves, learn to interact with peers— and those abilities and connections can be fruitful and useful but aren't accurately captured by your chosen major.

The truth is, a degree is more a representation of your opportunities in life and your ability in the moment to tick off the boxes. It doesn't necessarily make you better at doing certain things, and it may not necessarily give you practical skills. Having a degree from a bastion of higher education doesn't necessarily confer you a lifetime of skills. It's one way to measure your past accomplishments. It always has been, but I believe it's even more true now.

For example, in the medical profession, for example, they recognize this potential flaw, and they actually make you retake the boards on an ongoing basis. It's the same idea behind continuing education credits required in other professions and other recertification processes. You have to prove that you still know what you're doing and that you're learning to navigate the way the field is changing. It's a recognition that what you may have acquired fifteen years ago does not automatically equip you for the current challenges of your industry.

It's your skills that really matter.

Even degrees themselves are essentially a construction of a number of different skills or courses aimed at skills acquisition, a series of building blocks of set capabilities. Whether it is a degree or a badge, or whether you need recertification, ultimately, skills are the core piece of what organizations around the world seek and sometimes need to define, refine, and redefine. Suppose you want to find the best person for a job. In that case, somebody who is actually the most skilled or successful may not be the person who is willing to stay within the pedagogy of a set degree but instead applies other skills to achieve success.

It doesn't mean degrees are no longer necessary, but there are companies who are now acknowledging that you may have experts working in a particular field who don't actually have a college degree. There are a slew of stories, and we've all heard them: hackers or highly talented entrepreneurs—the Mark Zuckerbergs, Steve Jobs, and Bill Gates of the world. Companies that limit the hiring of people to those with a formal degree and neglect to understand the true skill set of a person may be leaving a lot of great skills or talent on the table.

When I was at a prior employer, we were interviewing for a very specialized skill set, and the person was truly outstanding. You could just tell from a conversation with her. She had deep skills, understanding and the knowledge we needed, plus years of experience, despite not having a college degree. Did we give her the job? I wish.

We chose not to hire her because that degree was a basic requirement. Now at my current employer, IBM, we have, over the past five years, consciously taken a different approach. Skills take precedence. As of 2020, 50 percent of our US job openings do not require a four-year degree, and that method is scaling globally. And we're okay with that, because they have the skills they need to fulfill the job.[1]

That's in a corporate setting.

I want to make the distinction here between business and non-business—the difference between the informal and the formal economy is so vast. There are so many examples of where this might affect one differently than the other. For many different tasks that are discrete, I think we're increasingly finding that you can source that anywhere: a virtual assistant doesn't automatically need to have attended secretarial school. There are any number of people in the Philippines, for example, who could be very capable virtual assistants without having attended a secretarial school or other formal training.

The gig economy—essentially, decentralized talent —further breaks down value in terms of skills over employment history or degrees.

Traditionally, companies expected their labor to be completed by full-time employees, on site. More than a year of pandemic restrictions, which sent many workers home, has helped to change that perspective. In a way, it was already happening. We're starting to see more and more companies using part-time employees, independently contracted specialists, gig, or traditional employees who don't have to be present to perform well.

In the future, we may see even more of a movement toward large, decentralized networks of people with specialized skills and subject matter expertise. Think about how Nike operates. They don't make any products. They design and market them. Someone else manufactures those sneakers you buy, right down to the laces.

In the same way, that network of talent coming together to deliver on an organizational outcome is very possible and already coming to fruition in many cases. Think about consulting project teams or construction teams—even oil drilling teams. They come together for a particular purpose rather than by a particular employer. They approach a task as a group, and they execute it. It happens all the time.

Rapid advancements in technology, changing demands for skill types, and speed of transformation have created a pressing incentive for employers to shift toward a labor model that prioritizes flexibility and access to short-term, gig economy workers. This creates a tremendous burden on HR teams as enterprises must efficiently discover, hire, train, and retain talent to meet those rapidly changing needs. Focusing on the LEGO blocks of skills is a streamlined way to tap into a global pool of talent. This pool includes gig and independent workers, as well as those who may be perfectly capable but currently limited to the informal economy.

There are many jobs, which—that can be discretely defined in terms of the skills or outcomes required—and detached from a degree. This taps into the origins of the socioeconomic implications we see. Degreed people get jobs, even though many others are just as capable. You pay money for a college degree; that's part of the opportunity cost of going to college versus getting a job at minimum wage. You're instantly democratizing skills by delinking the college degree as a determinant of value. That's just in the formal economy.

Basically, the theory is that you can decouple skills from degrees; this has always been the case in the informal economy. Blockchain can give you access to those skills in a way the internet is already doing, except with better outcomes. The key, though, is going to be how we define a skill in a way that actually makes it translatable and verifiable.

This is all part of societal evolution and the evolution of work. Automation, as we all know, replaces a lot of people. We've seen that since the Industrial Revolution. There are so many instances of where technology is replacing humans in ways we may not have ever considered feasible, or acceptable. That's the push we see toward handmade or artisanal items. There may be people who don't like spices that have been ground in an electric blender; they want to know it was made and mixed by hand. On a larger scale, though, technology is here to automate. That's going to continue in perpetuity. Since the days of Henry Ford, we've seen tasks broken down into discrete pieces of work that individuals would do. He capitalized on specialization, where you would do one task and one task only. That trend of making skills into discrete boxes and then using technology to enable them isn't going anywhere. In fact, it's accelerating.

The disruption of jobs is significant because the skills required change at an increasing pace while other skills are being automated. It's a constant churn and constant change, which is creating a skills gap that is widening all the time. A 2020 global survey by McKinsey & Company showed that nine out of ten executives and managers either face skill gaps or expect them to develop in the next five years. Only a third of respondents said their companies are prepared to navigate workforce disruptions. A third also said their organizations have launched "reskilling" efforts.

On top of that, we're projecting that 65 percent of kids in elementary and middle school today will be trained for jobs that won't exist when they graduate.

It's not that educational systems aren't trying to keep up. For example, there is a new course at the University of Thunderbird on Space Policy. Multiple schools that are following suit, with courses on space law and ethics in space and sustainability in space. Consider the topic of blockchain. In the past few years, more schools have offered courses on this emerging technology. As each skill set reaches a point of prevalence or usefulness, educational systems respond.

We can also consider the changing curricula of IBM, which has a learning credentialing network. There are a number of organizations that have already collaborated to implement a blockchain framework for education in veterinary medicine: Ethos and VetBloom work with IBM to develop solutions for the Association of the American Veterinary Medical Colleges, the American Association of Veterinary State Boards, the American Animal Hospital Association, the International Council for Veterinary Assessment, IDEXX, and Mars Veterinary Health.[2]

In this consortium in the veterinary sphere, we see a proactive approach to using a blockchain to create a learning credential network, which can serve as a meaningful model for the efforts of organizations like the Sovrin Foundation.

That's one example where using blockchain as the system of record to capture job skills and credentials makes it easy for people to use.

What we're finding in the real world is what many of us already intuitively know: It's hard to provide access to opportunities for many sections of society. It's also really hard to authenticate skills because sometimes you may have people who are actually great coders, for example, but did not get access to college. The power of having a credentialing authority to verify the skills, to record a person's pathway of skills, learning, and accomplishments will enable a more equitable playing field, as will the self-sovereign controls inherent in the blockchain the Sovrin Foundation aims to foster.

The idea of linking curricula and coursework with actual STEM jobs is an approach that IBM helped pioneer in 2011 with a brick-and-mortar career and technical education model called P-TECH (Pathways in Technology Early College High school), now with more than three hundred schools in twenty-eight countries. These schools offer teens from socioeconomically challenged communities the opportunity to earn both a public high school and free, STEM-related community college degree within six years. Industry partners like IBM—from a variety of industries, not just IT —provide mentors, paid internships, and job interviews. P-TECHs build on typical public high school curricula with STEM skills sets that map to entry level and mid-level STEM job roles involving IT help desk, website design and cybersecurity, and many more. Industry partners affiliated with a given P-TECH perform skills mapping that connect and enhance the local curricula with skills needed for specific job roles.

Since P-TECHs are not yet in every community, IBM launched Open P-TECH in the spring on 2020 as an extension of the idea that teens should be exposed to STEM concepts and technologies directly related to job roles—as well as human-centered, professional workplace proficiencies like collaboration, presentation and critical thinking. IBM SkillsBuild for Students introduces learners to everything from cybersecurity, AI and cloud basics, to exposure to graphic arts and careers in sustainability. Open P-TECH, now called IBM SkillsBuild for Students, provides learners with the opportunity to earn the same type of badges available to IBM employees who successfully complete IBM's continuing education courses online. These certifications signal to universities and prospective employers that the learner understands key concepts and mastered skill sets that might relate to specific roles. Blockchain is not currently used for SkillsBuild for Students credentialing, but if it is applied, it will make learning even more accessible and verifiable.

Whether it's a 150-year-old higher education institution or a company taking education into their own hands, the issue of credentialing and verifying remains. Official transcripts or even services like notary publics have played the role of providing a stamp of approval or some level of validation for documents. However, all, unfortunately, are easy to forge.

What we need is a solution that is *uneditable*. Blockchain provides trustworthy verification and validation because it builds a distributed, digital ledger of all transactions, with a history that cannot be altered. It creates critical immutability, with timestamped, cryptographically signed blocks that can be tracked all the way back to the first block in the chain. For educational institutions and accessibility, the potential is game-changing. Consider a 2015 paper by Open University, which suggested applying blockchain to online learning opportunities through smart contracts to shift learning toward personal development and away from money—essentially decentralizing learning contracts. Those contracts could translate into what we might think of as educational currency, building a chain of learning, a set of credentials that could be easily shared with employers or others, to demonstrate personal skill sets and education. It could also help shape more customized curricula by creating a learning time-line to demonstrate each student's history and help educators create next steps.

That's just one approach. Blockchain can also open the door to educators tailoring learning to students, as well as using peer-to-peer networks. Students themselves can share information and contribute toward others as well as their educa-tional institution, which can provide financial advantages for those students and support innova-tion in educational settings. It will also make educational institutions more flexible—a pressing need in a world where industries are routinely disrupted and new in-demand skill sets are emerging continually.

Consortiums of academic institutions and organi-zations have already launched solutions, still under development, to create permanent, validated records of learning, skills certifications, and qualifications, with an eye toward addressing the dynamic job market to which I just alluded. Those organizations recognize the need to reduce skills gaps. Currently, there are more than seven hundred thousand unique credentials hiring managers might be seeking at any given time. Combined with the reality of resume fraud, this presents a complex and ongoing problem for growing companies that need to speedily increase their workforces.

The changes are happening quickly across the educational sphere, and that speed is a necessary component for a rapidly changing world, the Fourth Industrial Revolution, as the World Economic Forum helped define: "The First Industrial Revolution used water and steam power to mechanize production. The Second used electric power to create mass production. The Third used electronics and information technology to automate production. Now a Fourth Industrial Revolution is building on the Third, the digital revolution that has been occurring since the middle of the last century. It is characterized by a fusion of technologies that is blurring the lines between the physical, digital, and biological spheres."[3]

As a consequence of that ongoing transformation, over 350 million people will actually have to shift their occupational categories by 2030. How do we, individually, respond to that? How can talent management and other executives plan, change, and adapt in response?

Let's start with an employer, because that would be the person who needs to find somebody with the right skill set. If you have a place where you can search for these new or newly in-demand skills, along with the advantage of a trusted blockchain network, you can cast a wide net, across a global talent exchange.

A digital passport with hash keys can provide access to demonstrated learning, training, and skills. Somebody who actually wants to apply for that job can share information, to show the skills and certifications they have earned, even if they are from five different institutions or learning platforms.

Thanks to self-sovereign identities, those candidates can select the keys they want to make visible to the hiring manager. They can be very selective in what they show and the access they provide. When a recruiter looks at those keys and that passport, they know that they're authenticated because they're on the blockchain.

As a potential employer, I am also trying to map those credentials and skills to actual jobs, and because it's all digitized, it's far easier for me to work with a framework that is already in place. It's a smarter, more secure version of what we might do as opposed to a hodgepodge way by poking around the internet. It's also far more trustworthy.

The unalterable trail of verified historical building blocks provides immutability. The ability to verify the genesis of information from certifying agencies provides provenance. Having access to verified information submitted by a decentralized network —not one sole source of truth (such as the applicant herself or himself)—provides accuracy and efficiency.

Immutability. Provenance. Efficiency. Access.

In a world where the basic unit of work becomes skills—not degrees and not job descriptions— blockchain allows for speedy connections to skills and talents needed by today's organizations to succeed and grow sustainably.

SEVEN

Blockchain and Contingent Staffing

AS WE ALL KNOW, the world of work is changing swiftly, especially when it comes to traditional work arrangements. Much of the move toward contingent staffing was already in play before the pandemic and its immediate, temporary shift toward remote work. Many of these remote workers embraced the flexibility of working from home and weren't ready to give it up when offices began to reopen, and those workers have added to the ranks of the gig economy army, choosing to be their own bosses.

Consider the so-called Great Resignation. The US Bureau of Labor Statistics shared in 2021 that four million Americans quit their jobs in July of the same year, with the highest rates landing among mid-career employees.[1] Are those workers really not working at all? Of course not. Where are they going? Many discovered that they like working remotely, and they want a better work–life balance. Contingent work, at least on the surface, holds promise for both of these drivers.

That's just one recent example of the ways our traditional concepts of work are being upended— and one way that contingent staffing is expanding and will continue to grow. It's for this reason that I call it the **Great Reckoning**. It's a positive thing if we examine it closely and understand it from a broader lens. It's reflective of the mood and ability of our global community that helps us take stock of how we need to organize work more effectively by taking advantage of the benefits of technology.

A 2020 Staffing Industry Analysts gig economy report[2] indicates that about a third of US workers —fifty-three million people—are contingent workers, meaning they work through a temporary employment contract, often with multiple companies. That includes consultants, independent contractors, freelancers, and temps, or temporary contract workers. Notably, that figure doesn't even include the global talent exchange that is now open and available to those in hiring positions. The true scale of gig economy work is much higher and will likely continue to expand.

We're finding an entire generation of people who don't seek lifetime employment, shifting our view of what a career means and contributing to an entire ecosystem of gig work or contingent work, as larger corporations might term them. And there is a viable place for them. As organizations find that skills and capability requirements are changing rapidly, the flexible workforce fits right in. Our technology doesn't always fit right in, however.

Managing this process requires defining the work or project, defining the skill sets needed, and identifying the candidates who match. Then there is checking the work, keeping track of time, paying the contractor, managing contracts, and raising a purchase order. There are any number of software applications designed just for these tasks, but software can only automate this back and forth of information. There are still a myriad of inefficiencies in the process and opportunities for error.

Anyone who has ever performed work as a contractor for multiple employers likely knows this kind of work requires constant documentation oversight: contracts, hours worked, projects completed, invoices sent, invoices paid, and more. And as anyone who has ever been tasked with processing the paperwork on the other side knows, things can get complicated very quickly, especially for organizations whose scope and temporary or contract employee roster is more than a few individuals. In many cases, large enterprises are juggling thousands of contractors, for technical and business services, and more. That boils down to a whole lot of paperwork.

Companies like Upwork, formerly Elance-oDesk, have seized the opportunity to create a market platform and help manage the business arrangements. The company currently has fourteen million registered freelancers and five million registered clients; three million jobs are posted there annually, worth a total of $1 billion. In that model, work projects are posted on the platform, and freelancers vie for the jobs, submitting quotes if they are selected for review. Freelancers can rack up stars and ratings like social media-leaning platforms, such as TripAdvisor and Airbnb. The documentation required to manage this is pretty significant, especially if a company employs a large number of contingent staff. Blockchain is the ideal answer to spheres where the need for trustworthy and accessible documentation and contracts—and potential discrepancies—come together.

There is a blockchain solution specifically for this pain point with its Contingent Labor on IBM Blockchain.[3] That software tracks time sheets, purchase orders, and other records and secures verified approvals by all parties involved. Because it provides a shared, secure, and immutable digital ledger, it can relieve enterprises of the time and expense necessary for invoice reconciliation and for late fees incurred during the reconciliation process.

The company had been assigning teams to validate vendor invoices, with a cost per invoice attached, and then handling disputes with dispute resolution teams, which cost up to $1,000 each. The cost and effort involved quickly multiplied and eventually added up to 1.5 percent of the company's annual expenses. In China, tech firm

Tencent, which developed the social media platform WeChat, developed a blockchain invoicing tool in 2019. In its first year, the software had managed invoices worth nearly USD$1 billion.[4]

Blockchain can take the many transactions involved in contingent hiring, managing, and paying contingent staffing and puts them on the shared ledger so that everything can be linked to exactly what is happening in real time. Imagine gig work without the constant tracking and back and forth, waiting to get paid, or waiting to process payments after they go through internal approval processes. In a shared ledger model using blockchain, we associate all these contingent or gig workers to a specific purchase order or job requirement. As time and expense accumulate, every transaction is attached to the block related to that particular purchase order. There is no back and forth, no matter how much you're layering on information. The information is validated; there is no more inefficiency that comes with information flowing from person to person.

Of course, some would argue that there is a limit to the scale and complexity of projects and work that can be tackled this way. It also can create a bottom-dollar market where those in economically disadvantaged situations can be taken advantage of or can shape a system where credentialed, qualified candidates can't compete with low-ball quotes.

With the gig economy and proliferation of flexible work, more and more companies are deciding to use contract labor, or they may have been using contract labor for a long time. At the same time, more people are seeking flexible work, perhaps an entire generation of people who don't seek lifetime employment but instead want to tap into this growing ecosystem of gig work.

The concept is not new; consultants have been employing it forever, and the opportunity is greater than it's ever been because of skills gaps and the emerging in-demand needs required by enterprises in a disruptive environment. Contingent work is particularly suited to immediate, skills-based needs. Specialists may be critical but only required for a short time. Or specialists your organization requires immediately may be working primarily on a freelance basis.

Because it can be so challenging to manage the contingent and contract labor process—finding contractors with the exact right skill set and checking their credentials all the way to making sure they complete the work and get paid in a timely manner—a blockchain solution is the best candidate for creating an amicable, affordable, and speedy way forward.

The issue with software that has been proposed is that it focuses primarily on the exchange of information. If mistakes are inputted, mistakes will be outputted. It doesn't provide an ultimate answer. Blockchain takes all those transactions and, by putting them on the shared ledger, links everything to exactly what is happening in real time. You don't have to rely on people to process and input information. The shared ledger model attaches each contingent or gig worker to their specific purchase order or job requirement. As time, work, and expenses move forward, all of that is tracked and attached to the block related to that particular purchase order. It removes the back and forth and builds a chain of verified blocks that cannot be altered.

The results are plentiful and promising: removal of reconciliation costs, ease of payment, fewer payment disputes, less cumbersome audits. Everything is recorded speedily, in real time, and those records are trustworthy.

Significantly, it doesn't create an altered or new process for contractors to work through. They have an interface to process and handle transactions. Blockchain doesn't change how they do their work; it only minimizes the amount of back and forth and the need for reconciliation. It improves the outcome without altering the way work happens. It makes life and record-keeping far simpler and more efficient for both the contractor and the company that relies on his or her work. Think of it as an upgrade: going from a fifteen-year-old gas guzzler to something with a much more efficient engine of a totally different build. It's going to run smoothly, faster, and cost you less time and money in maintenance and fuel. You still have to get in your vehicle and drive—the same as you always have—but you can spend the time, energy, and money previously tied up to get you where you want to go on keeping up with, or surpassing, others in your particular industry.

We've talked a lot about blockchain's role in connecting us with new talent in a world full of potential—much of it, as yet, untapped, and that includes workers in the gig economy. We haven't dived into the way it can smooth and streamline, or altogether remove, the mountains of paperwork we process for employees who are already part of our team, as part or full-time staff. Critically, this also applies to the heart of retaining those valuable teammates: how well we care for them.

Entire industries are already built around the pain points and paperwork of payroll, employee benefits, insurance, and pensions. The global outsourced payroll industry is projected to reach $38 billion by 2027.[5] In-house administration costs can vary, but a global average cost for employers can be as much as $194 annually, per employee. Timeliness and accuracy are paramount. It's long been a time-intensive process and one that grows increasingly complex with each new hire. For companies that employ hundreds or thousands of people, it's an ongoing and intricate machine that must be kept well-oiled and constantly maintained. It is a constant and ongoing pain point, one many of us have always assumed just comes with the role of keeping people employed and on our team. But there are so many efficiencies to be accomplished.

Think about what can happen when things go awry. Timing of payments can range up to eight weeks for some employers. If a payday is missed, it can cause serious cash flow problems for employees and their children or other dependents. Late payments can lead to financial instability or expensive, exploitive payday loans. Imagine an employee trying to hold her household together and missing a mortgage payment because payroll was delayed for a week; her credit score would be affected for the next decade. A missed paycheck might launch a cycle of hardship for some of your employees, which is exactly the kind of environment you don't want to create. You want to offer your employees stability and safety; it's part of your moral and social (and legal) contract with them.

Blockchain can be a game changer in these spaces where people, documentation, verification, and financial transactions converge. When you think about talent management operations in an organization with a wealth of employee transactions—a few hundred or a few thousand people— blockchain provides a critical benefit: ensuring the fiscal health of the workforce, both in payments and in investments. On a blockchain, payments and investments are shielded from cyberattacks and other digital vulnerabilities in a scenario where a high volume of transactions, and oversight that is stretched to the human maximum, might otherwise leave an open door to fraud, theft, or errors.

How might we see pensions and retirement plans affected? Some believe blockchain could offer unique solutions to retirement planning, with unique flexibility. Employees of the millennial generation, known not only for changing jobs, and with them pension investments, more frequently but also for investing more diversely, also stand to benefit from the security of blockchain-based investing systems. Blockchain makes the administration of pensions less time- and cost-intensive. Down the road, we will likely see organizations considering cryptocurrency for pensions because it would be easier to administer and easier for employees to execute those frequent changes and diversification, with records and data available instantly. Version history, timestamps, and signatures would all be trackable and trustworthy.

Employees could be paid immediately, and employers would trim hefty administrative costs of performing payroll every two weeks. No more waiting for payroll to process. No more employees watching their bank accounts anxiously, hoping their paychecks make it in before the next big bill comes due.

Instead, blockchain would provide a tidy, trackable, accurate, and simplified means to administer employee benefits, pensions, and insurance in different blocks. Such a system wouldn't bring these critical operations to a halt when it's time to update a legacy system. And when it comes time to make changes to pensions or benefits, employees and employers could simply use smart contracts. Everything stays on the system; everything works the way it should and when it should. No more endless back and forth; no more unnecessary delays.

Empowered by blockchain, similar benefits could be applied to a distributed workforce. It may even reduce the need for benefits packages for permanent, contracted employees and associated employees. We could reimagine benefits packages for short-term contract workers, including employees in communities without strong social safety nets who might gain access to benefits such as health insurance and pensions. The outcome could be better results for all types of workers and greater flexibility and opportunity for companies in need of in-demand talent. It's a win-win on many fronts.

EIGHT

Blockchain Challenges and Risks

TO TAP into the transformational potential of
blockchain, we need to proceed with our eyes
open, and we need to work together. Three core
strengths of a viable blockchain—anonymity,
immutability, and distribution—also represent
potential challenges. The good news is, if we can
be aware of these from the outset, we are better
positioned to address them. Here's a high-level
look at those three attributes, which can present
both strengths and weaknesses:

Blockchain anonymizes information through the
use of a hash (an impossibly long string of
numbers) so cryptic that it provides nearly impene-
trable security, so long as the end user doesn't
inadvertently release that one-and-only key, a pass-
code that can never be reset.

Related, blockchain's immutability means information can't be reversed. Every block added to the
chain, even if it's made in error or created by

someone looking to do harm, remains in perpetuity.

The technology's level of distribution and decentralization means it's not controlled by a government agency or a private company, which provides freedom from overreach and potential oppression, and avoids reliance on outdated or outpriced technology. It also means there is a barrier of standardization and a lack of regulation and oversight and, in the same token, it won't reach its full potential without broad adoption.

In reality, some of these barriers presented are no different from the process of adopting other significant innovations. Some of our most powerful tools also pose dangers and risks. All of these can be managed depending on how they are implemented and who is using them. Think of the internet as a strong analogy. There is the issue of anonymity, knowing for sure that the people you're interacting with are who they say they are, and the corresponding measures that have evolved to provide enough security for most users to feel safe managing bank accounts online or making purchases.

As with the internet, there is the issue of distribution and access. Broadband is, more and more, being seen as a necessary piece of infrastructure. Nations and even rural areas in the United States without reliable internet access are unquestionably at an economic disadvantage; a public, distributed, and decentralized blockchain would help ensure greater accessibility.

And we all know people who've used poor judgment in the way they use the internet—everything from accidentally sharing selfies to compromising their own personal financial information on a social media post. Worse than poor decision-making or a lack of understanding of the public nature of the internet are the bad actors who take advantage of security vulnerabilities. Paramount to a safe, public blockchain will be leaders and early adopters who make integrity the heart of what we are shaping together.

The primary and greatest challenge of moving forward cohesively and thoughtfully is simply creating a greater understanding of what blockchain can do. We've discussed throughout this book the ways it can dramatically increase efficiency and lower costs, allow enterprises to expand, grow, and take advantage of a world of opportunity and burgeoning industries, and create greater accessibility and even greater equity when it comes to offering opportunities in a global talent exchange. Few people, at the outset of the World Wide Web, had any concept of how it would shape our lives at home or work or among industries across the globe. As with the internet, blockchain holds the power to connect us and reshape how we move through our lives, from our first few years of school through the sunset of an exciting career and beyond. It can open possibilities for enterprises that want to expand and grow and extend the economic benefits of that growth to individuals who are not already connected and plugged into existing silos. It truly represents another level of human development, not dissimilar to our explorations of space—from the moon to Mars and beyond.

In the same way as we might if we were co-exploring the galaxy, we want to be sure we're operating alongside people we can trust. It's going to take experience, navigating through missteps, and people who are willing to put in the time and do the work to erect the framework, advocate for standardization, and build out the infrastructure with existing historical data. It's no small task, but no worthwhile or game-changing outcome ever is.

Interoperability

For a public blockchain to succeed, we need players with the right intentions to step forward and take the lead, and we also need to reach a critical mass before the technology will be widely useful. We've seen progress among small consortiums, and as those networks grow and connect, some of this will happen naturally. Leaders in education have already made steps in this direction, as well as companies with solutions for contingent staffing or its partnership in veterinary education. Of course, financial markets have already experienced the impact of a blockchain system via Bitcoin. That's an arena where there is real value to be gained. We need people to see the significant value of its application elsewhere. We need leaders who see the vision, and we need adopters who are willing to roll up their sleeves and get to work. To reach global interoperability and truly cultivate the benefits of blockchain, we need a wide variety of platforms, across industries and institutions, to be able to talk to each other. We need terms, identifiers, and processes that allow different people and organizations to speak the same, streamlined language.

This will require setting standards and pushing for their implementation, not just among those organizations your company interacts with but across the spectrum and across national and international boundaries. Consider careers as a use case. Interoperability when it comes to building a career or discovering and hiring talent means those of us in the labor and education markets will have to agree on ways we will share, issue, and verify credentials and use them in a coordinated manner throughout all layers of this emerging technology. To be effective, interoperability needs to happen on the technical, structural, semantic, and organizational level.

Semantics presents a clear challenge, but it's navigable if we can define terminology—again, speak the same language. The organizational side presents a more complex barrier because it involves legal frameworks and engrained business processes. These will have to be considered in depth and dealt with through a genuinely collaborative approach.

Scalability and Testing

While reaching a fully viable blockchain requires a critical mass of adopters, it also brings up some unknowns. What happens when it reaches full scale? The beauty of blockchain is that it allows for swift scalability, and it's designed to allow for greater security than any other technology we've employed in our connected world thus far. The barrier is that it has not yet been tested on the expansive levels it was created to achieve.

The Financial Stability Oversight Council (FSOC), a US government organization, has raised some concerns over the ongoing expansion of blockchains and their future.[1]

We've described blockchain as a series of buildable blocks, much like LEGO kits, except these would be for structures that are unlimited in size. The very nature of this technology is that it allows for additions and greater and greater scale. Every transaction is a new brick or block in the chain; it builds up and out and never contracts. The layers just continue to build on the previous information infrastructure. Every time we use a blockchain, it grows a little bit. Data sets will constantly increase. The more the chain scales and increases in distribution, the more it adds value.

With this insight, the FCOS has expressed concerns that our society is approaching new, untested terrain through blockchain, and it is. As history has proven, the price of adopting new innovations is accepting risks and learning from experience. In this case, we're still building experience and we haven't yet seen how a full-scale blockchain might operate in the real world. Security breaches and fraud are a primary concern, and so far, none have risen to the level of extensive changes, which is good news, but still requires a watchful eye, by regulators and by blockchain leaders.

In Europe, the European Parliament (through the paper titled "Blockchain and the General Data Protection Regulation"[2]) also examined these issues at length. There is dissonance between some of the existing guidelines of the General Data Protection Regulation (GDPR) and the way blockchain technology operates. The first issue is that the very decentralized nature of blockchain eliminates the ability of one agency or a single data controller to provide redressal or rectification. The second is the fact that blockchain's attribute of immutability, which is designed to increase trust in the network, also makes it difficult to alter or erase data as desired by the owner, and as required by GDPR's Article 16 and Article 17, respectively, to change data and erase personal data.

While blockchain can provide immutability, that feature is also the one that needs to be understood and managed actively as networks are set up. This is, of course, because the compounding effect of an error that is recorded as a transaction is significant and can be problematic.

The standards of GDPR will also become more relevant.[3] GDPR was implemented in the European Union to raise the level of security to how information was handled. As we operate in a more digital world, these principles and standards will become more relevant and will need to evolve to support the basis for how we use blockchain globally.

The use of blockchain to manage digital passports and talent passports may enable attainment of these standards, but specific solutions built by different groups or consortiums need to be reviewed and understood from the lens of technical design and governance. This is because blockchain is just a type of technology, and when deployed, may have many versions with different rules and governance mechanisms.[4]

Without the right protections and oversight, blockchain holds some of the same dangers we face online. Spoofers and ill-intentioned users. Hackers. Even those spreading alternate versions of reality. Consider the damage that might unfold if someone created a parallel version of a blockchain node, except with inaccurate and harmful information, or if a hacker found a way to input inaccurate and harmful information onto the legitimate blockchain. Because blockchain draws its strength from distribution and operates by consensus instead of a single controlling authority, that node could, in theory, continue to grow. Because blockchain is immutable, that information could not be reversed or erased (though additional chains can provide validated clarifications or explanations). All of that will have to be considered as we build this framework. None of these underhanded tactics are new, but security measures will be more important than ever as blockchain becomes widely adopted and more connected in various aspects of our lives and businesses.

Security Protections (and Concerns) Through Anonymity

A foundational element of blockchain's safety and security is the hash: a string of numbers that provide an individual's "key" to accessing his or her personal information. That's in addition to a public key to allow others—educational institutions, employers, and the like—to access it. That private key is a one-and-only hash that cannot be replaced if someone else discovers it. Possession of the key and ownership of digital identity are inextricably linked. This creates an "endpoint vulnerability" and will require thoughtful education to end users on how to store and save their keys without opening the door to hackers and information thieves. It's the same vulnerability of personal information that already exists through computers and mobile devices, which are susceptible to malware and make for easy targets. Individual protections and safety measures can address this, but the importance of taking those steps must be communicated clearly and cannot be understated.

Likewise, from the standpoint of an enterprise, company leaders need to be vigilant about who accesses their system and the information moving in and out of it. Third-party solutions—think smart contracts or blockchain integrations—already have emerged and will continue to emerge. The security of a company's blockchain implementation will rely on having trustworthy vendors with their own secure systems and protocols for ensuring that personnel maintain the highest level of security and don't pose a threat.

All of these steps are nothing we don't already face, and they all are manageable on a small scale or in-house, but the true power of a public blockchain lies in its potential for broad, global connection and integration. That's the direction we're headed, despite the concerns and the risks. To make this work well for all, we need bright minds, understanding, integrity, advocacy, leadership, and vigilance.

NINE

Broader Implications

THE WORLD of work as we know it is already transformed from the environment many of us launched into when we began our careers. Most of us work with people across time zones, countries, and continents without thinking too much about the connectivity or accents. Most of us work among teams that have moved beyond the preliminary drivers of labor arbitrage and outsourcing.

Over the years, organizations have come to realize that there are more important reasons to look for talent around the world—reasons of pure skill, deep expertise, humbling drive, and purpose. Like Natasha's.

∼

NATASHA'S VOICE QUAVERED. She was older now, but felt she was ten years old again, trying to staunch the blood from her mother's head.

Natasha and her eight-year-old brother, Sam, had hammered on the kitchen door for fifteen minutes begging Papa to stop beating Ma.

"Why does he beat you?" Natasha gasped.

Sheela looked at her little girl sadly, blood clouding her vision.

"You need to study. Don't worry about me. You have a math exam tomorrow. Go. Study. Don't think of all this."

"Those kitchen tongs were heavy. They're made of iron, like a hammer, you know?" Natasha told me, more composed now. "He beat her with many things and hurt her in different ways. He had never beaten her on the head with it before. Maybe he was too drunk to know what he was doing."

THE PANDEMIC CATALYZED the need to make space for remote workers, building out remote teams and managing, in general, with offices closed or working through some sort of hybrid model.

The cube farm is out. Working with teams we may not see in person is in.

Looming larger than that, though, and already building steam before the pandemic's pressure to allow employees to work remotely, something more influential is at play. Never before in the modern workforce have we seen so many contract workers become part of the way companies oper- ate. The tidal wave of gig work flows hand-in-hand with the new dynamics of skill-based work. Needs for new skills arise quickly; gig workers offer a stop-gap solution. Companies want to seize opportunities to grow. Instead of time and money-intensive hiring and onboarding practices, they can peruse one of the many platforms set up to connect contractors with companies who need them.

On the other side, workers are discovering and valuing more the ability to shape their own work schedules, set their own hourly rates, and move among different clients rather than becoming a member of the 9-to-5 club and putting in their forty years, with their career trajectories tied closely to the ambitions of a single company. We've talked about the ways blockchain can help make this happen and benefit both sides of the equation by streamlining documentation and contracts and helping to avoid discrepancies and missteps.

If you're an employer with access to blockchain, you can authenticate skill sets. You know who you're working with. It opens up access to that whole world of talent in a safe, secure, and verified manner—and it opens up an avenue for you to bring people on for specific tasks and skills that are already validated. The wonder of this is that it also can help people make choices that meet their needs and design a lifestyle that suits them better.

As finances grew strained, Sheela called her brother, distraught, hoping he would let Natasha stay with his family. So ten-year-old Natasha went to stay with her cousins for the next five years.

"Our poverty forced my parents to send us to live with my maternal uncle's family. I woke early each morning to cook for myself as my aunt refused to let me eat the food cooked for the family."

When she got back from school, Natasha swept the floors and cleaned the bathrooms. There was other abuse too. Afterward, Natasha showered and went back to her books. She had to leave. She knew there was a job somewhere out there in the world for her. She just had to find it. She just had to win it.

~

THE GIG ECONOMY gives everyone options. As opposed to being a full-time homemaker or a publisher or a consultant, people can choose to have multiple professions. They can be a doctor and a writer, or they can be a doctor and a baker. A healthy gig economy, empowered by blockchain, allows you to parse out the skills because each skill can be tracked in a different way and validated appropriately.

It gives us so much more flexibility within the global economy, all built on a concept as simple as LEGO blocks. It's a far more effective approach to jobs that have become so complex. If you're a publisher, for example, you need to know how to work with authors and manage them, but you also need to understand social media and the process for every step of the publishing and marketing process for both print and online publishing. We see it across industries. With rapidly changing technologies, connections, and advancements, each particular job has evolved into something much more complex. When we think about skills as LEGO blocks, every job can be deconstructed into these individual blocks. Blockchain helps us validate each one.

It helps employers hire contractors or employees whose verified skill set blocks match those specific needs. Workers with a variety of skill sets can put them to work where they can bring the most value and reap the greatest benefits; no longer do they need to toil away at positions that are a match for only a few of their passions. The federal government has led the way in this blended employee/gig worker frontier: traditional full-time employees, contract employees, gig workers, and others on some form of contingent worker contract all work together.

It's easy to see how this shift could benefit the individual, but we also need to consider how these changes shape an organization overall. How do you motivate and focus teams when you have a mix of traditional employees and contract employees? Modern teams might have employees working in an office, a number of employees working at home on a mix of schedules, and gig workers who are available a set number of hours. On top of that—and this is great news and also a great challenge—these workers can be culled from more diverse ideologies, identities, locations, and backgrounds than ever before.

LATE ONE NIGHT, her numbness ripped apart by the new scale of abuse, Natasha ran from her uncle's house. Unable to be silent anymore, she fled home to her parents.

"Soon after I returned, Pa died. Unmourned. He was forty and basically drank himself to death. Fortunately, he didn't kill Ma in the process."

Their wealthy family on both sides, ignored them and didn't help at all, while Sheela and her children tried to make ends meet.

Sheela, Sam, and Natasha started afresh.

"I needed to make money as I was the head of the household now at sixteen."

Natasha knew that her best, most monetizable skills were academic. She had to become an engineer, like her mother dreamed.

"I knew that through all of this, if I kept my grades up, I would be able to get a merit-based, free seat for college."

BLOCKCHAIN, working on the LEGO block model of matching validated skills for employers and talent, enhances the capabilities that will allow for a mix of employees and non-employees. The teams that work together, in turn, are going to become much more blended than we've seen in the past and much less loyal to a corporate identity or an organizational identity.

Those of us who work in talent or manage teams will have to adjust accordingly and find ways to unify and align people who are very diverse in terms of thought, political ideology, working and professional environments, and personal experiences. This will be the next great challenge, and it's a worthwhile one.

From a social justice and equity perspective, the tools blockchain offers will enable us to expand opportunities to a far broader audience of global talent. If that's something you care about, this offers the means to create a more fair, equitable talent marketplace, whether we're talking about traditional employment, contingent staffing, or gig work. Next up, we'll need to think about how to engage, inspire, and connect these more diverse teams, especially when much of the actual work may be completed in a virtual environment. Those of us working in talent management have much work ahead, but it's full of promise. The future of work has so much potential. We just have to pull together and approach it with intention.

We have to keep people at the heart of what is happening. If we're moving forward (or backward) to something more like the Henry Ford model, with people valued for their particular skills, how do we ensure that we're treating them as whole people? That will be one key to keeping workers engaged and on board. The other is to make it easy for them to gain the value and flexibility they're looking for in the first place. More and more people want to pursue their passion, but they don't want to commit their entire career to one particular employer. Organizations are also seeking more flexibility. We may need to allow for temporary connections, where workforces and teams may swarm together to work on a project and then disperse. That doesn't mean relationships can't be built; making the process work the way it should is one step to creating a positive working environment that gig workers will be happy to return to the next time you need them. We need to be open to working outside the rigid structure and hierarchies that once shaped our working lives.

Sam had so many ideas to make money, to make a living, pay for college. "As women, my mom and I were more limited in what we could do and stay respectable within our community. I worked so many different jobs. I sang and danced in musical orchestras. I did voice overs and even acted in a movie. I got paid to make announcements at events. I learned to be a great emcee. But my best job was the cable TV payment collection. I went house to house, collecting money. Eventually I was able to give my mom some of my cable routes, and that supplemented her sewing money."

The memories and glances of Natasha's small town were painful. So, Natasha studied. Sam's and her brilliant academics and sports records helped them get support from their teachers and friends. But she needed a degree to get a good job.

❧

WE DO SEE some of this happening in consulting organizations today, where people come together as project teams that are selected based on the skill sets that people bring and the requirements needed. Once the project is finished, the team disbands and moves on to other work.

In some ways, this provides a useful match to many of the dynamics we've covered: organizations need new skills, industry disruption is happening across the globe, and the rate of change is outpacing anything we've seen before. Being able to find the new skill set, quickly, may mean the difference between growth and lost opportunities, or falling out of the race altogether when a world of competitors are at your heels.

Oracle has applied for a new patent related to the blockchain—one that harnesses the crypto technology to optimize workflow, called "Managing highly scalable continuous delivery pipelines," based on the use of blockchain technology to track contributions to a work process or product, allowing for performance recording and access monitoring.

We need complex solutions to complex challenges, and we need them quickly. We need people, and the right people at the right moment. To go a little retro for a moment, it's almost as if we're working with a gigantic Rubik's Cube. Work today is a puzzle. The ground is shifting underneath our feet, and we need to keep up. We have to match the talent with the most immediate need. Sometimes this is needed to pull together immediate solutions, and sometimes to line things up in a way that frees up other, existing matches to make progress elsewhere in the overall organization. Shift one area, though, and another may need our attention. We have to keep moving to make everything line up the way that works best for everyone: the company and the people who make it viable and help it grow.

This isn't just the case for consulting firms or companies that provide services. This happens in more concrete areas, too. Think of the oil and gas (or any) industry—with its modern-day gold rushes of booms and busts—and its project-based work against the backdrop of long-term objectives. Think of the project-based work inherent in publishing, in the arts, or even in education. Much of the work we do lends itself well to a different structure than 9-to-5 office jobs with a set-in-stone hierarchy. It's going to happen more and more across industries and countries. For talent managers, we haven't been, and won't be, looking at benefits that fit neatly into those outdated structures. We can't just offer strong pensions and investments. We need to look at employee engagement. Business leaders need to consider much more than they used to. How are they using social media to engage teams? What kind of support do they offer for virtual working environments? How are they connecting people and sharing the joy and recognition of big accomplishments? How do you build a sense of community for them? It's far more nuanced than it ever has been before. Leaders will have to consider their value system. What are your expectations, and how can you accommodate teams with diverse work styles? Do you have people who like to work 9 to 5? Or do they like to work all night and then not work for the next two weeks? Those are the real practical issues that we will be challenged with.

These are the conversations that need to happen. Clear expectations and clear communication will be critical.

Organizational Structure

On top of the rise in gig work, of course, is increasing automation. Much of our transaction processing and documentation processes now can be managed by machines, and that will only continue. This new picture of work should be one that allows more people to do the work they enjoy and excel at, with skills matched to each project, and less of the drudgery that used to come with clocking in to work. A robot can do the box checking and processing. If a particular project demands a different type of skill than an individual already has, that aspect of the project might be assigned to an expert.

What does this mean for what we thought we knew about the office? It can mean great things. You're using people's skills in the most valuable way, which is solving important problems instead of paper pushing. It also means organizations are going to have to start thinking about organizing and operating in domains of expertise, which is how consulting firms operate. It's less about process or transaction-oriented domains and more about identifying solutions and getting to the end goal. As opposed to the way we run a particular process, it's finding the right technology to run it for us and letting our teams guide the strategy, flex their expertise, and make decisions.

The other element at play here is that its work is becoming opt in or opt out, on some level. The whole concept of the gig means that the worker gets to say yes or no. Initially there was this backlash and hand-wringing around the loss of job security, but now we see that people may actually want to line up twelve-hour days for six months so they can run off to spend the winter as a scuba instructor in the Caribbean. People want options. The once golden ideal of spending twenty years working long days and weekends to become a partner isn't appealing to everyone anymore. The corner office is no longer the ultimate goal. People want freedom to live and work in a way that suits them best. They want to be able to choose. We are moving away from a one-size-fits-all model to something that can be customized.

Optionality is becoming very important. That will affect leadership. It will affect team structure. It will affect the employment experience you offer as a whole. And it gives the organization more options, too. If you're looking, even globally, for that one in 7.7 billion, you may never find him or her, despite how our tools evolve. You're probably never going to find the world's best hacker who is also a Harvard MBA grad. If you try to find both in one person, you're going to find neither. You have to decide which one is important or else ask why you can't go with two people, whether that's two full-time employees or a mix of gig, contingent, and traditional employees. Then, once you find your people, you're going to need to craft an employment experience or an organizational capability that caters to the needs of these diverse people and what they want and need.

Diversity covers a lot of ground. We can also think about it in terms of what workers want. They won't all be looking for the same experience. It also speaks to learning and thinking differences. Think, too, about those who are on the autism spectrum or may not have been considered employable. They bring very valuable skills to the economy, and blockchain allows us to tap into those. Marginalized skill sets, whether individuals from around the world or neurodiverse people who may not attend job fairs or ship out traditional resumes, have a better chance at connecting with opportunities because employers can start thinking about jobs as a composite of different skills. If we are more open to differing work arrangements than we were previously, we can figure out ways to take advantage of the opportunity to include those who might otherwise have been overlooked.

NATASHA SAID, "My teacher Karishma really helped me during those years. She is LGBTQI and was an outlier in our community. Karishma's courage to be open about who she was, is astounding. She was always graceful, elegantly dressed and my first mentor."

At this point, the tenth grader was old enough to be out and about on her own.

"I studied under street lamps and in friends' homes where there was food and light available freely. Since we could only afford one new dress each year, most of my wardrobe came from my Muslim friends who donated clothes each Ramzaan. I ate, studied, and was clothed by all these people around me. My teachers helped me a great deal, especially Karishma who helped me improve my English. It's funny how these things lead to a chain reaction of support. Since I was able to speak English, it made me more bold, more articulate.

"I was brave enough to get a meeting with a very reputed teacher in town to be coached in math. My mother gave me the grocery money to pay for his fees. But, he took me on

without fees because he was impressed by my ability to make my case. Gaining one skill helped me gain another."

DISRUPTING work hierarchies can help make us more equitable in many ways; it can also make us stronger and more capable of solving complex problems. The value of multidisciplinary and cross-functional teams has been highlighted before; think of tiger teams, an approach first introduced by the military. When big problems come up, they would come in and crack them. The difference there is that the rest of the teams would continue working on the new, improved product or service until the next time they hit a bump in the road. What we're seeing now is a democratization of problems. This isn't just about bringing in a special team for a special occasion. A multidisciplinary approach, with input from diverse individuals who are not trapped in immoveable structures, offers a more nimble and effective workflow.

The Role of Leadership

In addition to navigating increasing job complexity—and project complexities—leaders in a blockchain-enabled environment will need to keep a sharp eye on recognizing and valuing those diverse needs and strengths. Strong leaders will become more important than ever, and I don't mean "strong" in the sense of authoritarian. The future will call for something quite the opposite. The most pressing requirements of leaders will be competence and integrity. I don't think you can have one or the other.

Part of that competence will be capably over-seeing the Rubik's Cube of talent, having a full grasp of each job, and each project's complexity and dynamics. Being able to break down projects into skills required and matching those skill blocks to the right talent, and then bringing it all into a cohesive, functional whole, is no small task. Blockchain and AI will be important tools, but only when they are intelligently and thoughtfully employed. That capacity for whole-picture vision will become more important than ever as we work in domains of expertise rather than set processes; working without a set hierarchy doesn't mean there is no room for leaders. They will just have to be more agile and more knowledgeable.

Only when you have deep expertise in your field will you be able to exercise true integrity of thought. If you're manning a mission into outer space or trying to colonize the moon, you need to know that the people who are with you on that colony have the skills that will be most critical. You don't want to be stuck looking down at Earth and thinking about training someone to make sure your air seals were properly checked or main-tained. You need to know what is required before you go and choose and engage the right talent before you go. We'll need empathetic leaders who are good listeners, leaders who see what people need. We also will need leaders who have integrity of competence and integrity of courage to do what is right.

Natasha's high grades and brilliant academic track record gave her the opportunity to go to college at reduced fees. This was the first step in Natasha's journey outside her world. Her optimism and ability to connect with people helped her navigate her chosen path of HR very well.

"I have my own consulting firm now, which I started after getting my master's degree at Rutgers and working in Corporate America. And only because I was able to get my college degree back then."

Natasha works with business leaders around the world to help them figure out what they need to ensure equity and equal opportunity. She is a keynote speaker at leading conferences and won awards for her work in diversity.

"There is a lot of work to be done. Corporates provide a lot of opportunity and mobility. The impact of a good job is far reaching, as you know," she said. "But the truth is that we need to continue to work toward it. Leaders need to operate with a lens that provides understanding of these issues."

IN THE FUTURE, the role of the leader becomes more like a coach calling plays. Teamwork is not operating necessarily by consensus, or at least not by consensus only. If you're on a team, it doesn't mean you don't have a voice, but you do need a coach to pull everything together, moving players where they can achieve their personal best and putting the team as a whole in the best possible position to make a goal or win the game. Coaching is more than charisma; the best plays are executed only when the coach is coming from a place of deep competence. Research tells us that it's the servant leader, those who put the mission above their own ego or personal gain, who can build sustainable success for a team.

It's not only what the coach says or does on the field but also how she or he inspires each person to play the best game of his or her life. A "strong" leader sees her role as uplifting the entire team. That's the ultimate goal, and it's why researchers like Jim Collins, advisor in business and social spheres and the author of the classic management bestseller *Good to Great*, tell us that the ultimate leadership style combines extensive executive capabilities and willpower in addition to humility. That quality is, and will be, much more important than charisma or followership.

Like any trailblazing technology, blockchain offers us a portal to new possibilities. Those will also require new and deepened responsibilities and responsible leadership. The wonder I remember experiencing as a girl at my father's workplace, the way science and technology could solve basic human needs like hunger, is still there. Blockchain can offer us that transformative power: opportunities for marginalized people and people with marginalized skill sets, avenues for companies to find the skills they need, and validation tools to streamline hiring processes so more people can access a viable livelihood. As we explore this new territory, we need to make sure our ethics and moral compass keeps up. We need to continue to build human trust as we shift validation and verification to blockchain processes. We need to be more relationship-focused as we offer, and accept, new opportunities. At the end of the day, behind our technology, it's human intelligence and ingenuity that makes all of this possible; working together, we can extend the benefits to create a world full of opportunity—for everyone.

TEN

Conclusion

OUR NEED TO connect with each other is one of our most fundamental needs. And trusted connection is THE enabler to achieve all of our other fundamental needs. We trust, connect and collaborate, to work together, and be together—to feed ourselves, keep ourselves safe, gain comfort, and progress as a civilization.

Acceleration in our progress has happened when we have connected across geographies and barriers. And, our progress has always accelerated exponentially when we tap into diverse pools of talent. For example, there is evidence that the inclusion of women in the more formal workforce resulted in an uplift to the economy, and as more women joined the workforce, they helped make cities more productive[1] and increased wages.[2] Similarly, the inclusion of marginalized groups and communities into the economy will further accelerate growth.

If we are able to mobilize every kind of intellectual horsepower—men, women, veterans, immigrants, marginalized, neuro-atypical, gig workers —we will supercharge our global community and our global economy. Those (employers) who seek talent with whom to engage and collaborate benefit through knowledge and access to what's out there. And those (individuals) seeking to gain skills and deploy them to make their livelihood benefit from gaining information and access.

We can use blockchain to disrupt traditional ways of recruiting, learning and accessing opportunity. We have the opportunity to streamline processes, improve data integrity and access to verified information.

If we look around the leadership rooms of leading organizations in the world, we see a pattern of success in organizations when the leaders are more diverse.[3] And diverse, not from a purely ethnographic view, but also with diverse skills and experiences. The C-suites of leading innovators in pharma and technology companies are all filled by individuals who would have been unlikely candidates for the role a few decades ago. This shift has come not just from a mindset change but also from recognition that the optimal talent for the job need not come from the most adjacent geographical, ethnographic, or socioeconomic vicinity.

As we move into the Fourth Industrial Revolution,[4] we need to bring along large swathes of our global community who are not currently participants in this journey. We all need to recognize that we limit ourselves when we restrict ourselves from accessing the talent in marginalized talent pools and when we limit who can access opportunities. In the past, some of these limitations were due to lack of understanding, lack of data, and lack of technology. But not anymore. Everything we imagine is possible.

So then, as we gain more digital connectivity, what remains as the barrier? Our barrier will be the need to trust across our networks. The ability to understand provenance when it is less known, less storied, less branded. The ability to understand that a diamond is a diamond, even when less polished. And the ability to understand when it is not a diamond at all.

Blockchain, when deployed with integrity and good governance, has the potential to help us operate seamlessly with trust—across our communities, our world, and our universe.

Notes

Dedication

1. Bob Dylan, "Planet Waves," 1974.

Epigraph

1. Brihadaranyaka Upanishads (1.3.28). Translated from Sanskrit.

1. Our Connected Future

1. Mumbai, the city formerly known as "Bombay." It is the capital of the state of Maharashtra, and the commercial epicenter of India. Christened "Bombay" by its Portuguese claimants, it was part of the dowry of Catherine of Braganza, in her marriage to King Charles II and was handed over to the British in 1661. It was renamed as "Mumbai" in 1995. https://www.britannica.com/place/Mumbai/History

2. Kerala is situated in the southwestern end of the Indian subcontinent. The state with the highest literacy rate in India, it is noted for its achievements in education, health, gender equality, social justice, law, and order. https://www.kerala.gov.in/

3. https://www.technologyreview.com/2019/05/30/65724/how-a-quantum-computer-could-break-2048-bit-rsa-encryption-in-8-hours/

4. https://www.weforum.org/agenda/archive/space

5. https://www.matthewball.vc/all/themetaverse

6. https://www.history.com/news/who-invented-the-internet

7. https://www.fronticrsin.org/articles/10.3389/fbloc.2020.00024/full

8. https://www.ibisworld.com/global/market-research-reports/global-hr-recruitment-services-industry/

9. The nuclear reactor Cirus was built by Canada and used heavy water (deuterium oxide) supplied by the United States.

2. What Is Blockchain?

1. Satoshi Nakamoto, "Bitcoin: A Peer-to-Peer Electronic Cash System," https://bitcoin.org/bitcoin.pdf.
2. Haber, S., Stornetta, W.S. How to time-stamp a digital document. J. Cryptology 3, 99–111 (1991)
3. Grigg, Ian. (2004). The Ricardian contract. 25–31. 10.1109/WEC.2004.1319505.
4. R.C. Merkle, "Protocols for public key cryptosystems," Proc. 1980 Symposium on Security and Privacy, IEEE Computer Society, pages 122–133, April 1980.
5. R.C. Merkle, "Protocols for public key cryptosystems," *Proc. 1980 Symposium on Security and Privacy*, IEEE Computer Society, pages 122–133, April 1980.
6. BFT vs Proof-of-Authority:Applying the CAP Theorem to Permissioned Blockchain *Stefano De Angelis1,2, Leonardo Aniello1,2, Roberto Baldoni1, Federico Lombardi1,2, Andrea Margheri2, and Vladimiro Sassone2
    Research Center of Cyber Intelligence and Information Security, Sapienza University of Rome
7. https://www.hyperledger.org/
8. https://www.corda.net/
9. https://consensys.net/quorum/

3. The Universal Talent Exchange

1. https://www.worldometers.info/world-population/
2. https://www.ilo.org/global/about-the-ilo/newsroom/news/WCMS_627189/lang--en/index.htm
3. Hunter, John E., and Ronda F. Hunter, "Validity and Utility of Alternative Predictors of Job Performance," *Psychological Bulletin* 96, no. 1, (1984): 72–98, https://doi.org/10.1037/0033-2909.96.1.72..
4. Harvard Business School, Accenture, and Grads of Life, *Dismissed by Degrees*, 2017, https://www.hbs.edu/managing-the-future-of-work/Documents/dismissed-by-degrees.pdf.
5. Ibid.

4. Blockchain and People Data

1. Kerosene was called Ghaslet in Hindi—derived from its use to light lamps. It was also called "Rockel" in Marathi derived from "rock oil" and "Mann-enna" or earth-oil in Malayalam.

2. In India, "bai" is commonly used as a respectful suffix for women in Hindi and Marathi. It is also used as a synonym for "maid" in Mumbai.

3. *Neel* is a deep blue pigment found in the Lapis Lazuli. More recently, it's made artificially as a double silicate of aluminum and sodium with some sulfides or sulfates.

4. *Phulka* is a round wheat bread, like a roti. They are rolled thin and roasted over a flame to puff it up.

5. https://www.ncvhs.hhs.gov/wp-content/uploads/2014/05/050113p3.pdf

6. https://sovrin.org

7. https://www.ibm.com/support/pages/frequently-asked-questions-ibm%C2%AE-digital-health-pass-users

8. https://www.technologyreview.com/2019/05/30/65724/how-a-quantum-computer-could-break-2048-bit-rsa-encryption-in-8-hours/

9. https://www.weforum.org/agenda/archive/space

10. https://www.matthewball.vc/all/themetaverse

11. Feynman RP. Simulating physics with computers. International Journal of Theoretical Physics. 1982

12. https://www.mdpi.com/1099-4300/19/6/240/htm

13. https://www.ncbi.nlm.nih.gov/books/NBK538701/#!po=3.33333

14. Bub, Jeffrey, "Quantum Entanglement and Information," The Stanford Encyclopedia of Philosophy (Summer 2020 Edition), Edward N. Zalta (ed.), URL = <https://plato.stanford.edu/archives/sum2020/entries/qt-entangle/>.

15. https://www.wired.com/story/nasas-plan-to-turn-the-iss-into-a-quantum-laser-lab/

16. https://thequantuminsider.com/2021/08/04/quantum-technology-in-space/

17. https://carnegieendowment.org/2019/04/25/implications-of-quantum-computing-for-encryption-policy-pub-78985

18. https://www.oecd.org/sti/inno/space-forum/measuring-economic-impact-space-sector.pdf

19. https://www.spacefoundation.org/2021/07/15/global-space-economy-rose-to-447b-in-2020-continuing-five-year-growth/

20. https://www.uschamber.com/technology/the-space-econ-omy-industry-takes
21. United Nations Space Objects Index. https://www.un-oosa.org/oosa/osoindex/index.jspx?lf_id=
22. https://news.mit.edu/2021/newer-nimbler-faster-mission-venus-search-signs-life-clouds-sulfuric-acid-1210
23. https://blogs.nasa.gov/artemis/2020/10/28/lunar-living-nasas-artemis-base-camp-concept/
24. https://www.planetary.org/space-policy/maven-cost
25. https://www.vanityfair.com/news/2017/06/neal-stephen-son-metaverse-snow-crash-silicon-valley-virtual-reality
26. https://www.matthewball.vc/all/themetaverse

5. Blockchain in Recruitment

1. https://www.prnewswire.com/news-releases/new-check-ster-research-shows-78-of-job-applicants-lie-and-66-of-hiring-managers-dont-care-301004406.html
2. https://www.hireright.com/PDFs/2021_Benchmark_-Global_Report.pdf
3. https://www.alliedmarketresearch.com/employment-screening-services-market
4. https://hbswk.hbs.edu/item/minorities-who-whiten-job-resumes-get-more-interviews
5. https://www.studentclearinghouse.org/nscblog/clearinghouse-ibm-and-learning-credential-network-members-join-with-the-u-s-commerce-department-to-launch-pilot-to-align-education-with-cybersecurity-jobs/
6. https://mediacenter.ibm.com/id/1_doynqihl

6. Blockchain in Learning

1. https://www.ibm.com/impact/be-equal/pdf/IBM_Diversity_Inclusion_Report_2020.pdf
2. https://www.ibm.com/blogs/blockchain/author/patrick-welch/?mhsrc=ibmsearch_a&mhq=blockchain%20veterinary%20%20education
3. https://www.weforum.org/agenda/2016/01/the-fourth-industrial-revolution-what-it-means-and-how-to-respond/

7. Blockchain and Contingent Staffing

1. https://hbr.org/2021/09/who-is-driving-the-great-resignation
2. Staffing Industry Analysts, "The US Gig Economy," 2020, https://www2.staffingindustry.com/Research/Research-Reports/Americas/The-US-Gig-Economy-2020-Edition.
3. CIO, "IBM Blockchain Automates Contract Labor Process," February 3, 2020, https://www.cio.com/article/3518780/ibm-blockchain-automates-contract-labor-processes.html.
4. CoinTrust, "IBM Rolls Out Blockchain Tool for Casual Labor Agreements," February 4, 2020, https://www.cointrust.com/market-news/ibm-rolls-out-blockchain-tool-for-casual-labor-agreements.
5. https://www.reportlinker.com/p05961083/Global-Payroll-HR-Solutions-Services-Industry.html?utm_source=GNW

8. Blockchain Challenges and Risks

1. https://fiscal.treasury.gov/fit/blog/five-quick-takeways-on-blockchain.html
2. https://www.europarl.europa.eu/RegData/etudes/STUD/2019/634445/EPRS_STU(2019)634445_EN.pdf
3. https://www.gdpreu.org/gdpr-requirements/
4. https://www.europarl.europa.eu/RegData/etudes/STUD/2019/634445/EPRS_STU(2019)634445_EN.pdf

10. Conclusion

1. Amanda Weinstein, "When More Women Join the Workforce, Wages Rise—Including for Men," *Harvard Business Review*, January 31, 2018.
2. Amanda L. Weinstein, "Working Women in the City and Urban Wage Growth in the United States," April 3, 2017, https://doi.org/10.1111/jors.12336.
3. https://www.mckinsey.com/~/media/mckinsey/business%20functions/organization/our%20insights/delivering%20through%20diversity/delivering-through-diversity_full-report.ashx
4. https://www.weforum.org/agenda/2016/01/the-fourth-industrial-revolution-what-it-means-and-how-to-respond/

About the Author

Elizebeth Varghese is a futurist, people & technology strategist, and senior executive who leads and helps transform organizations around the world. She is among the top experts and inspirational leaders of 2022 per The HR Gazette. In 2021 she was recognized as one of the Outstanding 50 Asian Americans in business, and in 2020 she was a global Top 100 Influencer in HR Strategy and Analytics. Elizebeth is the Global Leader for Talent and HR Strategy Client Services at IBM. She is also an active board member at South Asian Youth Action, a nonprofit providing after-school programming, education, and college support. She is on the Council of Advisors at the SETI Institute, which works with NASA and other space agencies to explore, understand, and explain the origin and nature of life in the universe. Elizebeth has MBAs from both the Columbia Business School and the London Business School, as well as a master's in personnel management from the Tata Institute of Social Sciences and a bachelor's in pharmaceutical sciences from the University of Mumbai. Elizebeth is also a bestselling author for her contribution to *Significant Women: Leaders Reveal What Matters Most*. She lives in New York City with her husband and two daughters.

Made in United States
North Haven, CT
21 January 2022

15081434R00108